Sir Paul Vinogradoff

THE VINOGRADOFF INSTITUTE
DICKINSON SCHOOL OF LAW
PENNSYLVANIA STATE UNIVERSITY

ON THE HISTORY
OF
INTERNATIONAL LAW
AND
INTERNATIONAL ORGANIZATION

COLLECTED PAPERS OF
SIR PAUL VINOGRADOFF

Edited by
William E. Butler

THE LAWBOOK EXCHANGE, LTD.
Clark, New Jersey

Copyright © 2009 by William Elliott Butler (1939-)

ISBN-13: 978-1-58477-953-7 (hardcover)
ISBN-10: 1-58477-953-5 (hardcover)
ISBN-13: 978-1-58477-987-2 (paperback)
ISBN-10: 1-58477-987-X (paperback)

Lawbook Exchange edition 2009

The Lawbook Exchange, Ltd.
33 Terminal Avenue
Clark, New Jersey 07066-1321

Please see our website for a selection of our other publications and fine facsimile reprints of classic works of legal history:
www.lawbookexchange.com

Library of Congress Cataloging-in-Publication Data

Vinogradoff, Paul, Sir, 1854-1925
  On the history of international law and international organization : collected papers of Sir Paul Vinogradoff / edited by William E. Butler.
    p. cm.
  Includes bibliographical references and index.
  ISBN-13: 978-1-58477-953-7 (cloth : alk. paper)
  ISBN-10: 1-58477-953-5 (cloth : alk. paper)
  1. International law--History--20th century. 2. League of Nations. 3. Vinogradoff, Paul, Sir, 1854-1925. 4. Law teachers--England--London--Biography. I. Butler, William Elliott, 1939- II. Title.
  KZ3295.V56A2 2009
  341--dc22
                                    2009005281

Printed in the United States of America on acid-free paper.

CONTENTS

Introduction   v
-William E. Butler

Sir Paul Vinogradoff: A Biographical Sketch   15
-William E. Butler and V. A. Tomsinov

INTERNATIONAL ORGANIZATION

The Legal and the Political Aspects of the League of Nations   37
The Realities of a League of Nations   45
The Covenant of the League: Great and Small Powers   55

HISTORY OF THE LAW OF NATIONS

Historical Types of International Law   61
   I. Historical Types of Law   63
   II. Greek Cities   75
   III. The Jus Gentium of the Romans   87
   IV. The World State of Mediaeval Christendom   101
   V. The International Relations of Territorial States   113
   VI. Modern Developments   129

BIBLIOGRAPHY

Towards a Bibliography of the Published Works of Sir Paul Vinogradoff
-William E. Butler   147

Publications Untraced
-William E. Butler   200

Personal Archives 200
-William E. Butler

Selected Personalia 201
-William E. Butler

INTRODUCTION

Pavel Gavrilovich Vinogradoff (1854-1925) is well known in Russia principally as an historian and abroad as a legal historian and comparative lawyer. Few in either Russia or abroad are aware that Vinogradoff also wrote on public international law.

Vinogradoff was a natural candidate as an individual after whom an Institute devoted to research on the legal systems of Russia and other Independent States of the former Soviet Union should be named. The Vinogradoff Institute, presently at the Dickinson School of Law, Pennsylvania State University, was originally established in 1982 at University College London. Members of the Vinogradoff family warmly welcomed the decision to name an Institute in his honor, for Sir Paul Vinogradoff remains the sole Russian jurist to be elected to a Chair of History in Russia (Moscow State University) and in England to a Chair of legal history (Corpus Professor of Jurisprudence, Oxford University), as well as to the Imperial Russian Academy of Sciences (St. Petersburg) and The British Academy (FBA). He and his career truly represented a bridge between the Russian legal community and the Anglo-American legal community.

Vinogradoff left Russia on 21 December 1901 in protest against a refusal of the Russian Government to accept his proposals for a reform of Russian universities. Taking up residence in England, he was elected to the Corpus Chair at Oxford in 1903, being well known and regarded there for his pioneering learned contributions on medieval English legal history. He had initially achieved fame in England in 1884. While at work in the Public Record Office, The British Museum, and the libraries at Oxford, Cambridge, and Cheltenham, he discovered previously unknown documents, among which was a Note Book of the thirteenth century on the basis of which the noted English jurist Henry de Bracton (d. 1268) composed his treatise on the laws and customs of England. Vinogradoff published notice of his find in the *Athenaeum* (19 July 1884). This created a sensation at the time, was duly authenticated as being what Vinogradoff supposed it to be, and remains one of the great landmarks in the history of English law.

Vinogradoff was a prolific scholar who published several major treatises, numerous articles and reviews, as well as translations of important works. Most were addressed to aspects of legal theory, comparative legal history, and, during the First World War and events leading to the Russian revolutions of 1917, to Russian affairs generally. The great majority of his publications up to 1917 appeared both in the English and in the Russian languages; that is, whatever he wrote and published in English, French, or German he himself also published in Russian journals. The Revolution of October 1917, to which he was vigorously opposed, made the practice of dual publication impossible. Virtually none of his post-1916 publications are known to Russian historians or jurists.

When, therefore, he was invited to the Netherlands in 1921 to deliver the public lectures at the University of Leiden on historical types of international law, he prepared a substantial text (70 pages) that has never been published in Russian and is known to few Russian international lawyers.[1] For him at the time one must assume that this was not a diversion from his principal scholarly interests. In 1920 he had published the first volume of *Outlines of Historical Jurisprudence*, the second volume of which appeared in 1922.[2] His reflections on international law were a natural extension of his researches on what he called "historical jurisprudence"[3] generally and cover from a slightly different perspective many of the subjects treated in his *Outlines*.[4]

---

1. See P. G. Vinogradoff, *Historical Types of International Law: Lectures Delivered in the University of Leiden* (Leiden, E. J. Brill, 1923). 70 p. Reprinted in *The Collected Papers of Paul Vinogradoff* (Oxford, Clarendon Press, 1928), II, pp. 248-318, and below.
2. The surviving manuscript of the third volume, never completed, reposes in the Vinogradoff Archive at the Harvard Law School.
3. For Vinogradoff, "historical jurisprudence" was the "study of the spirit of laws which aims at setting free a constituent element of prime importance – the dialectics of social principles in law". *Collected Papers*, II, p. 253.
4. His second lecture on "Greek Cities" was taken from volume 2 of his "Outlines."

INTRODUCTION

His work on historical types of international law is divided into six sections that reflected the cycle of lectures at the time. He began by identifying what he regarded as "historical types of law". In his view there were five types: (1) the tribe; (2) the city; (3) the Church; (4) the contractual association; and (5) the collectivistic organization. Without dwelling on these in detail, suffice it to observe that in his perception:

> ... the evolution of these groups is bound to assume some form of international intercourse, alliances, and federations. For purposes of defence as well as for trade peoples in the most varied geographical surroundings and in entirely different ethnographical combinations develop similar forms of self-help, arbitration, religious sanction. *Thus in every stage of civilization we meet with characteristic features of international law* [emphasis added – WEB].[5]

Applying this analysis to the Greek cities of antiquity, he observed that "it is a common error to suppose that the Greek world was deficient ..., that there could not be any talk of international law in societies sharply divided into a number of small republics". To the contrary, he argued, a closer study shows that "the world of Greek cities was particularly adapted to the development of a certain kind of international, or – to speak more correctly – intermunicipal relations".[6] Although he did not draw this comparison, the same might be said of the appanage princes in medieval Muscovy.

These Greek cities were not self-sufficient. They depended on trade and commercial relations with others; they received and regulated foreigners, they waged war, they sent heralds and couriers, they concluded treaties, they engaged in reprisals, they addressed issues of what in modern terminology is called the "conflict of laws", they conducted transactions under maritime law and recognized limits of maritime jurisdiction, they formed leagues and confederacies among themselves, they engaged in arbitration, they recognized the existence and applicability of customary

---

5. See below, p. 67.
6. Ibid., p. 75.

rules between communities, they developed procedural rules to deal with questions of inter-municipal justice, they applied sanctions to breaches of treaty obligations, among others. In short, the essential elements of what in modern times is called international law were well-known to and practiced by the Greek cities.

Roman law, in Vinogradoff's view, was an "agent of universal culture which results in the growth of a common law of the Roman Empire, the *jus gentium*".[7] The rules originated not in Roman legislation, but in the "juridical results of ideas elaborated by business practice and by professional analysis";[8] although not binding upon a Roman court in which such authoritative opinions were invoked, "they guided the magistrates in the same way as judicial precedents guide the bench in a trial under English common law". The *jus gentium*, he said, quoting Roman sources, may be defined as follows:

> ... that which natural reason has established among all men is observed equally among all peoples and is called the law of nations as being that law which is used by all nations. And so the Roman people uses partly its own and partly the law common to all men".[9]

When the world of Rome collapsed and fragmented, the institution which emerged to emphasize the unity of mankind was the Church, said Vinogradoff, and this was done above all through the concept of the *Civitas terrene* (earthly city). It was a powerful doctrine in its day whose implications were a world theocracy as a system of international order. Ultimately, the centrifugal forces at work made impossible the notion of a common unity embracing Christendom and the role of the Church as the final arbiter in the settlement of international disputes.

There emerged instead combinations of individuals in the form of territorial States, welded together by an awareness of na-

---

7. Ibid., p. 87.
8. Vinogradoff observed that Cicero traced expressly the development of the doctrines of good faith to the action of jurisconsults. Ibid., p. 93.
9. Ibid., p. 97.

INTRODUCTION

tional identity, or by regional competition, in both instances secular rather than religious communities. The roots of law were sought in the nature of man, a natural law based on principles of reason (law of nature) or on common consent (law of nations). Grotius wrote: "Natural law is so immutable that it cannot be changed by God himself. For though the power of God be immense, there are some things to which it does not extend …".[10] This kind of thinking, Vinogradoff suggested, led to the struggle and compromise of two principles: "that of natural justice derived from individual consciousness and that of the sovereignty in the territorial state derived from the requirement of social order".[11] A body of international doctrine grew up at the hands of Grotius, of Pufendorf, of Vattel "which formulated rules of international usage that had considerable authority even with the most arbitrary rulers".[12]

Vinogradoff stopped short of calling this law in the sense of lex (закон). But it was a form of natural justice which public opinion would endorse and therefore is "important and suggestive". Vinogradoff believed that the law of nations was greatly influenced in this period by the "transfer of private law conceptions into the domain of international law" under the influence of Roman jurisprudence:

> The cardinal doctrine of occupation is inspired by well-known precepts of Roman law. The concrete cases which presented themselves for discussion and settlement were chiefly suggested by the policy of discoverers, colonizers, and traders.[13]

Vinogradoff acknowledged that the "weak side" of public international law was the absence of compulsory sanctions, which "was evident from the first". This weakness could not be eliminated by a jurisprudence "which had renounced the concep-

---

10. H. Grotius, *De jure belli et pacis*, transl. W. Whewell (1853), Prolegomena, i.1; x.5.
11. See below, p. 123.
12. Ibid., p. 125.
13. Ibid., p. 128.

tion of a theocratic super-State and pinned its faith to the idea of territorial sovereignty". International law was "bound to recognize war as the natural outcome of self-help and its civilizing influence was directed towards preventing wanton atrocities and mitigating inevitable horrors". This situation was the outcome of a consistent application of the view that "a sovereign State is judge of its own case and is not subject to any legal superior".[14]

That brought Vinogradoff to "modern developments", which for him were in the immediate aftermath of the worst conflict the human race had ever witnessed: the First World War. He was a proponent of the League of Nations from the very outset. The conclusions set out in his lecture were modest, but insightful and of value at this moment in the evolution of the international system of the post-Cold War era:

> It seems clear that the contents of political and legal evolutions can not be brought under the rule of universal abstract formulas: the relations between Law and the State, between communities and their members, vary greatly in the course of history and have to be estimated by different standards. The only two universal and permanently fixed points in this respect are that individual as a given real being and society as a necessary real relation. The problem which every age has to solve is to find the appropriate combinations between the two.[15]

Vinogradoff's Leiden lectures were his last public utterances in printed form on the subject of the League of Nations. By the time they were delivered, the League was well-launched and even promising. Few have realized that Vinogradoff was a warm proponent of the League from the earliest postwar discussions leading to its creation. His views survive in three works, one an article which launched an auspicious Russian émigré publication in London, *The Russian Commonwealth*. His views are measured, juridically-based, and decidedly sober, especially considering what must have been a se-

---

14. Ibid, p. 129.
15. Ibid., pp. 143-44.

ductive temptation to see the League of Nations as a major instrument to be deployed against the Bolshevik Revolution in Russia. He does not accentuate this aspect of the matter; indeed, he offers no special hope to his Russian comrades-in-arms that the Russian Problem would be susceptible to resolution within the League.

He drew upon this article in the second essay on the subject which is published here for the first time. Who was the intended recipient of the manuscript for publication is not disclosed by the surviving archival materials. He did intend a much longer piece than the version published by importing segments of his previous essay into the text, which in itself suggests an important continuity of views as between autumn 1918 and early spring 1919.

The final item on this subject is a Letter to the Editor of *The Times*, which will have enjoyed a large readership in its day but has long since been forgotten by, if ever known to, the world of legal scholarship.

Whether Vinogradoff's interventions on the League of Nations issue played any role in persuading British official or public opinion as to the future configuration of the League and its powers, or in accommodating the nationality issue within the structure of the League, is a matter for independent study. He demonstrates in his writings, however, a mastery of the discipline; his are not the views merely of a concerned layman. His erudition in the law of nations was, not unexpectedly, on a par with his accomplishments in legal history and comparative jurisprudence.

We have preserved Vinogradoff's style of citation in the Leiden Lectures below.

W. E. Butler

SIR PAUL VINOGRADOFF:
A BIOGRAPHICAL SKETCH

William E. Butler
Pennsylvania State University

Vladimir A. Tomsinov
Moscow State University

Pavel Gavrilovich Vinogradoff[1] was born on 18 November 1854 at Kostroma, Russia, the eldest son of Gavriil Kiprianovich (1809-1885) by his second wife. His father, the offspring of a Suzdal priest, had graduated from the Main Pedagogical Institute in St. Petersburg and worked in Kostroma as a teacher of history, then as inspector of a male Gymnasium, and finally as the director of the Gymnasium. He was transferred to Moscow in 1855 as Director of the I Male Gymnasium and an increase in earnings, but with such a large family there were financial difficulties until in 1866 he was appointed to the post simultaneously of five girl's Gymnasiums. His mother, Elena Pavlovna (d. 1918), was the daughter of a veteran of the Fatherland War of 1812, Lt. General P. D. Kobelev (1793-1877).

Vinogradoff received his primary education at home, surrounded by three elder stepbrothers and, in time, four younger sisters and two younger brothers. Having mastered the syllabus of the primary classes at the Gymnasium, he excelled in his command of foreign

---

1. We observe the spelling preferred by Sir Paul Vinogradoff, who wrote as follows on 7 July 1916 to Winfred Stephens from his home at Court Place, Iffley, Oxford: "I confess that this question of transliteration of Russian names, though not difficult in itself, is complicated by tradition. At bottom such names as Metchnikov and Vinogradov should be spelled with a *v* at the end; but the transcription with *off* was introduced in the eighteenth century – I suppose under French influence; and in consequence a number of Russian names have, as it were, acquired rights of citizenship in this guise in various foreign languages. In my own case, I began to spell my name as Vinogradoff, and *off,* ever since I wrote my French exercises as a boy of six; and, as I have published a good many books at a later age under this form of the name, I should not like it to be changed". Quoted from W. Stephens (ed.), *The Soul of Russia* (1916), p. vii.

languages; French and German were quickly mastered and he began to study English from the age of twelve. Reading historical novels was a favorite pastime, those of Sir Walter Scott being preferred. In 1867 his parents placed him in the fourth class of the Fourth Moscow Gymnasium.

During his education at the Gymnasium, Vinogradoff formed his ultimate interest in history, especially the history of Western European countries. Graduating from the Gymnasium in 1871 with the gold medal, he enrolled in the Faculty of History and Philology of the Imperial Moscow University at the age of sixteen.

Among his university teachers, V. I. Gere (1837-1919), S. M. Solovev (1820-1879), and F. I. Buslaev (1818-1897) exerted the greatest influence on Vinogradoff. In his third year at University Vinogradoff undertook to write a medal work "On Land Possession in the Epoch of the Merovingians". On the basis of historical materials he for the first time drew special attention to the significance of law in the history of human society. Thereafter his studies of social history always were augmented by research into legal documents.

After graduating, Vinogradoff remained at Moscow University to train for the professoriate. In 1875 he was sent on scholarship to Germany in order to improve his knowledge of history and of legal history. At the University of Berlin he studied the history of Ancient Rome, visiting seminars of the noted historian Theodor Mommsen (1817-1903) and lectures on the history of civil law delivered by Heinrich Brunner (1840-1915). Spending the summer of 1876 at Bonn University studying ancient Greek history under the supervision of Arnold Dietrich Schaefer (1819-1883), he returned to Russia in the autumn of the same year. His contacts with German scholars left an enduring impact, and also gave evidence of his own aptitudes for an incipient encyclopedic approach to law and history and a capacity for detailed scholarship using original sources of the past. He later said the three greatest minds he had encountered and the three most powerful intellectual influences in his life were Mommsen, the Russian historian Vasilii O. Kliuchevskii (1841-1911), and the English legal historian and colleague, Frederic William Maitland (1850-1906). His first learned paper, written in German on the legal aspects of manumission, drew upon his studies in Berlin and launched his academic career.

Immediately upon returning from abroad he was offered the opportunity to lecture on Universal History at the Higher Women's Courses. With some interruptions Vinogradoff taught at that educational institution until 1888, when it closed down permanently. In Autumn 1877 Vinogradoff was invited to offer lectures on the history of the Middle Ages at Moscow University as an adjunct lecturer. In that same year he successfully passed his magister examinations and began to write the magister dissertation on the origin of feudal relations in Lombard Italy. The materials Vinogradoff gathered in the libraries and archives of Italy during the spring and summer of 1878.

P. N. Miliukov (1859-1943) was among those who attended Vinogradoff's earliest lectures and recalled:

> P. G. Vinogradoff perhaps did not satisfy us as a theoretician. But he impressed us with his serious work on aspects of history that were of interest to us on the basis of archival materials. And besides, he attracted us at once by the fact that, unlike Gere, he did not close himself off from us, was not condescending, did not enter into difficulties from our questions, but on the contrary, provoked them and treated us as workers on historical materials as he was. He came with a completed work on Lombard Italy drawn up on site using archives and in fact showing what one might expect from this. I do not recall precisely the sequence of his university courses: whether it was the Roman Empire or the beginning of the Middle Ages. But more important than his lectures were his seminars. Only from Vinogradov did we understand what real scholarly work means, and to some degree he taught us that.[2]

---

2. P. N. Miliukov, Воспоминания. Том первый (1859-1917) [Memoirs. Volume One (1859-1917)] (1990), I, p. 114. Other students recollections of Vinogradoff, of similar warmth and perspicacity, are found in A. A. Kizevetter, На рубеже двух столетий. Воспоминания 1881-1914 [On the Edge of Two Centuries. Memoirs 1881-1914] (1996), pp. 46, 59-60; M. M. Bogoslovskii, Историография, мемуаристика, эпистолярия [Historiography, Memoirs, Epistolaria] (1987), pp. 70-71.

In March 1881 Vinogradoff successfully defended his magister dissertation and published it in the same year. Prior to Vinogradoff's dissertation, the origins of feudalism had been treated almost exclusively using historical materials relating to the Kingdom of the Franks. This Russian scholar drew for the first time on materials relating to another country and succeeded in showing that in Lombard Italy, just as in the Frankish Kingdom, feudalism developed on the basis of the synthesis of elements of Roman and German societies. In his words, "the deep roots of feudal relations in Lombard Italy are secreted in the III and IVth centuries of the Roman Empire"; the "Roman system strongly influenced both the formation of the estates of feudal Lombardy, and the character of its economy".

In characterizing Vinogradoff's study, the historian D. M. Petrushevskii (1863-1942) wrote in 1930:

> the author coped brilliantly with his task and as a result a book has been received which is a true embellishment to Russian historical science, introducing the Russian reader to a true laboratory of European historical knowledge, acquainting him with the means and methods of historical research and from a broad perspective bringing him close to those great historical problems which then engaged the disturbed the scholarly world of Europe. One may say without exaggeration that the problems of feudalism have never been treated in Russian historical science in such a form, in the form of a wholly autonomous study encompassing all of the principal aspects of the feudalization process and with such thoroughness and clarity in depicting its social foundation. The book on the origin of feudal relations in Lombard Italy was in the full sense of the word a European book, and its author a European scholar, although the language in which it was written also obstructed its scholarly circulation in Europe, but the author thereof is a full-fledged citizen of its *respublica litteratum*.

After defending his magister dissertation, Vinogradoff was elected to and confirmed in post as a docent in 1881 in the Chair of Universal History. In the summer of 1883 Vinogradoff again went abroad, this time to England in order to collect materials for a doctoral dissertation on the social history of England in the Middle

Ages. Once more Vinogradoff decided to devote himself to the origins of feudalism, but this time to consider the example of English history. While at work in the Public Record Office, The British Museum, and the libraries at Oxford, Cambridge, and Cheltenham, the Russian scholar discovered previously unknown documents, among which was a Note Book of the thirteenth century on the basis of which the noted English jurist Henry de Bracton (d. 1268) composed his treatise on the laws and customs of England. Vinogradoff published notice of his find in the *Athenaeum* (19 July 1884). In 1887 Frederic Maitland published the Note Book of Bracton as a separate volume with an introduction confirming Vinogradoff's thesis regarding the authenticity and importance of the text.[3]

During this visit of nearly fifteen months, Vinogradoff came into contact with Sir Henry Maine (1822-1888), Sir Frederick Pollock (1845-1937), and Frederic Seebohm (1833-1912). His friendship with Maitland is said to have played a decisive role in the latter's decision to devote himself to legal history.[4]

In autumn 1884 Vinogradoff returned to Moscow and soon was elected professor extraordinarius of Moscow University in the Chair of Universal History. In 1889 he became professor ordinarius of the same University, and offered courses on the history of ancient Greece, the history of the Middle Ages, the history of jurisprudence, and others. A liberal by inclination, though by no means a radical, he was a gifted, if demanding, teacher and a fervent pro-

---

3. Maitland wrote that Vinogradoff "had learned in a few weeks more about Bracton's text than any Englishman has known since [John] Selden [(1584-1654)] died" – a remarkable tribute to Vinogradoff from the preeminent English legal historian.

4. Sir William Holdsworth wrote: "The combination [of Maitland and Vinogradoff] may be said to have put the study of the history of English law upon a new basis, and to have revolutionized the study of English social and constitutional history". The story of Maitland and Vinogradoff becoming first acquainted is complicated by divergent chronologies of when the event occurred. The matter is more or less sorted out in C. H. S. Fifoot, *Frederic William Maitland: A Life* (1971), pp. 59-62.

genitor of educational reform. He sought, in his words, "not only to form a school of historians, trained in the methods of western scholarship, but also to influence the progress of general education in Russia". He promoted an expansion of the network of elementary schools that would give every Moscow child access to a course of primary education. A series of elementary history textbooks were widely used and went through numerous editions.

From May 1886 to May 1887 the Журнал Министерства народного просвещения [Journal of the Ministry of Public Enlightenment] published the text of Vinogradoff's doctoral dissertation, and in 1889 it was issued as a separate book. In spring 1887 he defended the dissertation and became доктор наук. At the invitation of Oxford University Vinogradoff reworked his dissertation for publication in the English language in 1892 under the title *Villainage in England*; many critics regard this as his most enduring and lucid work.[5] He became recognized in Europe as a specialist on English social history.[6] In his preface he asked:

> Why should a Russian scholar turn to the arduous study of English medieval documents? We are still living in surroundings created by the social revolution of the peasant emancipation; many of our elder contemporaries remember both the period of serfdom and the passage from it to modern life; some have taken part in the working out and putting into practice of the emancipating acts. Questions entirely surrendered to antiquarian research in the West of Europe are still topics of contemporary interest with us.

---

5. Writing in the mid-1930s, Seagle commented that in retrospect this was "... his most brilliant book; it was generously described by Maitland as by far the greatest achievement in English legal history". See W. Seagle, "Vinogradoff, Sir Paul", in E. R. A. Seligman (ed.), *Encyclopedia of the Social Sciences* (1935), XV, p. 264.

6. "Anglo-Russian legal scholar and medievalist who was perhaps the greatest authority in his time on the feudal laws and customs of England". *The New Encyclopedia Britannica* (15th ed.; Chicago, 1991), XII, p. 381.

On his third visit to England in 1891 Vinogradoff delivered the Ilchester Lectures in Oxford, choosing as his subject "Slavophilism".

In 1892 he was elected a corresponding member of the Imperial Academy of Sciences.

During 1895 Vinogradoff worked in the libraries and archives of Norway, studying the texts of early Scandinavian law with a view to determining the extent of the latter's influence on the legal culture of Anglo-Saxon society. In the last years of the nineteenth century, besides teaching at Moscow University, Vinogradoff gave lessons at the Fifth Moscow Gymnasium. A reflection of his teaching exercises was a book issued in four volumes (1896-99) and awarded subsequently the Emperor Peter the Great Prize: *Книга для чтения по истории Средних веков, составленная кружком преподавателей под редакцией П. Г. Виноградова* [Book for Reading on the History of the Middle Ages, Compiled by a Circle of Teachers Under the Editorship of P. G. Vinogradoff]. The volumes were widely used and went through numerous editions. In addition, he was the initiator of the creation in 1896 of the Moscow Pedagogical Society attached to Moscow University and was elected its first Chairman; the Society discussed at its sessions the pace and problems of Gymnasium reform.

In 1897 Vinogradoff became a member of the Moscow City Duma, joining a group of Moscow University professors who in the period from 1893 to 1903 contributed immensely to school reforms. As Chairman of the Education Department of the City Duma in 1898, he succeeded in consolidating Moscow primary schools into larger and more efficient institutions, and also obtained for teachers a one-third increase in their remuneration. At the end of the nineteenth century, at the initiative of the Minister of Public Enlightenment, N. P. Bogolepov (1846-1901), intensive work was undertaken to reform education in the schools. Vinogradoff actively participated in this as a member of the Commission of the Ministry of Public Enlightenment.

The turn of the century in Russia was marked by student disturbances. Vinogradoff took an active part in settling conflicts between the students and the administration of educational institutions. As chairman of the Commission for Student Affairs, he worked out a specific plan of conciliation for bringing order to the universities and at the outset of 1901 submitted it to the then Minister of Public Enlightenment, P. S. Vannovskii (1822-1904). The Vinogradoff Plan was categorically rejected with rude remarks about the Commission having been chaired merely by a professor and not the rector of the University. As a sign of protest Vinogradoff resigned his position at Moscow University and went abroad. He declined the suggestion of the City Prefect, General D. F. Trepov (1855-1906), that he depart from Moscow secretly. From the day of his resignation until the day of his departure, the Vinogradoff home was thronged with visitors who came to pay him homage – professors, lecturers, students, school teachers, and on 21 December 1901 an enormous crowd of well-wishers attended the enormous Aleksandrov Railway Station to see him off together with his wife, three-year old daughter, and young son, Igor, born several months earlier. To those who gathered he made a brief and sober address, underlining the restraint which he had displayed throughout the education crisis.

After their winter of 1901-02 in France, at Cannes, the Vinogradoffs proceeded to England in the spring of 1902 and settled in Tunbridge Wells. Vinogradoff delivered two lectures at Cambridge on the "The Reforming Work of the Tzar Alexander II and the Meaning of the Present Development in Russia", while his friend Maitland worked on his behalf to secure an appointment at Cambridge University. In fact, the appointment proved to be at Oxford.[7]

In 1903 Vinogradoff was unanimously elected to the Corpus Chair at Oxford University.[8] He was now to see from the inside that

---

7. The Commission proposed, *inter alia*, that students be allowed to hold nonpolitical meetings in the presence of professors.
8. Maitland wrote to Henry Jackson on 13 December 1903: "I am living in hope that Pollock's successor at Oxford may be Vinogradoff. My own belief is that he will make a better professor than either Sir F. P. or Sir H. M. I wish much that we had him at Cambridge – but I felt last year that it was useless to say anything about him to Balfour as the Crown could hardly appoint a man to whom the Russian Government was (in effect)

of which nearly two decades earlier he had written about from the outside: Oxford through foreign spectacles.[9] In 1885 he had been impressed, first, by the "enormous wealth at the disposal of an English university". Evidence of the wealth included the buildings, the ability to spend, at the time, the staggering sum of £2,000 pounds a year on foreign books alone, and every college having its own library. Second was what he called an "aristocratic stamp" and the separation in England between liberal and professional education. In comments which proved to be prophetic in his case, he advanced an argument on behalf of the "seminar" system and its integration into the "regular course of university studies". Soon after his election to the Corpus Chair he acted upon his earlier impressions and suggestions, and the seminar became an integral component of an Oxford postgraduate education.

From that moment the scholarly interests of Vinogradoff were concentrated upon legal history, although he continued to write on the social history of England. In 1905 and 1908 he published two books on the Middle Ages in England: *Growth of the Manor*,[10] and *English Society in the Eleventh Century*.[11] His enthusiasm for educational reform left a lasting imprint upon Oxford University and eventually British higher education as a whole, for he introduced at once a method of seminar teaching unknown to that venerable University which combined history and law and generated an enthusiastic coterie of disciples. A direct outcome of the seminars was several seminal monographs on English legal history, including one of his own.

In 1906 Vinogradoff was elected a Fellow of the British Academy (FBA).

---

giving the sack". See C.H. S. Fifoot (ed.), *The Letters of Frederic William Maitland* (1965), no. 370, pp. 288-289.
9. Pollock commented: "Oxford has done no better since she adopted Alberico Gentile [(1552-1608)]".
10. See P. G. Vinogradoff, "Oxford and Cambridge Through Foreign Spectacles", *The Fortnightly Review*, XXXVII (1885), pp. 862-868.
11. Described by Seagle as "less an attempt at discovery than a coordination and sifting of existing views". Note 5 above, p. 264.

The first two decades of the twentieth century were the most productive periods in Vinogradoff's scholarly life. He wrote an entire series of articles for the eleventh edition of the *Encyclopedia Britannica* (on Anglo-Saxon Law, Comparative Law, Inheritance by Operation of Law, the rural obshchina, serfdom, and others); articles on Anglo-Saxon legal and political institutes for *Real-Lexicon des germanischen Altertumskunde*, and others in the *Law Quarterly Review* and elsewhere on the origins of feudalism, including in the *Cambridge History of the Middle Ages*.

From 1913 Vinogradoff directed the publication of a series of documents on the social and economic history of England, as well as becoming editor of the "Oxford Studies in Social and Legal History". He served as director of publications for both The British Academy and The Selden Society.

Various universities in the United States, Europe, and Asia regularly invited Vinogradoff to lecture on legal history. In 1907 he lectured on Ancient Law at Harvard University; in 1909 on the fate of Roman Law in Europe of the Middle Ages, at London University; in 1914 on the law of kinship in Calcutta, India; in 1922 on public international law at Leiden; and in 1924 at Oslo.

In Autumn 1908 and Spring 1910 Vinogradoff became a supernumerary professor at Moscow University, offering courses on the history of jurisprudence and on problems of social history of England in the Middle Ages.[12] At the same time he gave seminars on the Code of Theodosius and the reception of Roman Law in England and France.

---

12. He wrote on 20 December 1907: "To-day the deputation of the Faculty called upon me ... When the Dean had stated the request of the Faculty that I should join them again, I explained that I should like to try and combine one term's teaching in Moscow with my two English terms, but I would on no account give up my teaching in Oxford. They... expressed their satisfaction at the fact that I should be able to give three months in the year to Moscow". Quoted in H. A. L. Fisher, *Paul Vinogradoff: A Memoir* (Oxford, 1926), p. 45.

On 18 January 1914 the Imperial Academy of Sciences in Petersburg elected Vinogradoff as Academician.

Vinogradoff died on 19 December 1925 in Paris at the age of 71 shortly after receiving the degree of Doctor *honoris causa* from the University of Paris. Other academic distinctions conferred included D.C.L. (Oxford (1902), Durham [1913]), LL.D. (Cambridge (1905), Harvard (1907), Liverpool (1908), Calcutta (1913), and Michigan), Dr. juris (Berlin, 1910), and Foreign Member of the Royal Danish (1909), Royal Belgian, and Norwegian Academies, Corresponding Member of the Prussian Royal Academy (1911), of the Royal Academy, Bologna, of the Academy dei Lincei in Rome; and of the Society of Sciences, Lviv, Poland; Member of the International Academy of Comparative Law; Honorary Member of the American Antiquarian Society (1896); and Acting President of the Union of Academies, Brussels.

His funeral service at Paris in the Russian church was attended by French and Russian colleagues and pupils alike. Russian students bore his coffin from the church and he was cremated at Pere Lachaise. His ashes were interred at Holywell Cemetery in Oxford, his tomb being inscribed with the words of his choice: Hospitae Britanniae Gratus Advena.

While on a visit to Norway in 1897, he married Louise (d. 1934), daughter of Judge August Stang, whose own wife was an Englishwoman, Isabel Mary Newbold. A daughter, Helen, was born of this marriage in 1898 and a son, Igor Pavlovich (1901-1987). Although making his home in England from 1901, Vinogradoff maintained close links with his homeland. During the 1905 revolution he was in St. Petersburg and in 1906 was sounded out about accepting the ministership in public instruction by the new liberal government headed by Count P. A. Stolypin (1862-1911). He agreed to accept on condition that anti-semitic restrictions imposed on access to education be repealed[13] and declined the post when this condition could

---

13. At the time there was a 3% quota on the total number of Jewish students who could be admitted to the Universities of St. Petersburg and

not be unequivocally met.[14] He lectured as honorary professor at Moscow University in 1908, 1909, and 1911, resigning even these visiting appointments in February 1911 together with more than a hundred other colleagues when he found police spies in the lecture hall.

In the eyes of his Russian colleagues, despite frequent visits to his homeland, Vinogradoff was becoming increasingly a European in style and speech. In 1907 Vinogradoff met with a Russian parliamentary delegation which visited Oxford. Among the delegation members was his former student, V. A. Maklakov (1870-1957), who in his memoirs assessed the occasion and his former teacher as follows:

> Vinogradoff, with his views and with his Europeanism, could not live easily in Russia. And if we could not imagine Kliuchevskii outside Russia, we see Vinogradoff in Europe much more readily. On the contrary, it would not be easy for him to live in Russia not only with the Government, but with our society. He knew Europe too well, was too genuine a European, and does not recall that the failures and misfortunes of Russia happened not only through the fault of our authorities, but also through the lack of preparation, the lack of seriousness, of our society. He could not fail to feel for the liberation movement with its ultimate ideals, but he understood that "it is not easy to rectify a matter of centuries", that only "freedom" and "commonwealth" cannot at once relieve Russia from those habits which our unreasonable absolutism inculcated. Vinogradoff did not share the attractions of the Kadet Program ... If Vinogradoff had after 1905 remained in Russia, Russian party life would have ruthlessly passed him by without taking advantage of his talents as it passed by many of those who by their merits and services represented at the time the best part of Russian society ... Vinogradoff by his temperament and intel-

---

Moscow. The inability of Vinogradoff in earlier years to obtain a teaching position at Moscow University for Mikhail Gershenson left a deep mark on Vinogradoff and led to his seeking the abolition of these limitations.
14. A more recent version of this episode links the offer of a ministry to

ligence had outgrown the attractions and illusions of the infantile period of our political freedom, when the parties and their leaders not only worked to the benefit of Russia, but, in addition "played in Europe". Vinogradoff's departure for England during the constitutional restructuring of Russia was a simple coincidence, but it all the same was a symbol.[15]

For Vinogradoff the First World War promised a new era of moral and social regeneration for Russia. He wrote in 1914:

> It is our firm conviction that the sad tale of reaction and oppression is at an end in Russia, and that our country will issue from the momentous crisis with the insight and strength required for the constructive and progressive statesmanship of which it stands in need.

He labored assiduously during the War years in the interests of Anglo-Russian relations and a new liberalism in Russia. In 1916 he visited Russia again, acting as chairman of the Anglo-Russian Society and remaining on after the February 1917 Revolution.

Sir Bernard Pares (1867-1949) described him as being at the very back of every effort in England to promote the academic study of Russia. He was a member of the Liverpool School of Russian Studies, and in his capacity as External Examiner he examined the first British student to present Russian History as the subject for his

---

Vinogradov with an invitation made by Stolypin to A. I. Guchkov to become Minister of Trade and Industry, an appointment which Guchkov agreed to accept on condition that A. F. Koni become Minister of Justice and P. G. Vinogradoff become the Minister of Public Enlightenment. Stolypin had no objections, but Emperor Nicholas II, having originally agreed to Guchkov's appointment, reconsidered and Guchkov was not appointed. The candidacies of Koni and Vinogradoff were automatically removed from consideration. A. S. Senin, Александр Иванович Гучков [Alexander Ivanovich Guchkov] (1996), p. 22.

15. V. A. Maklakov, Воспоминания [Memoirs] (2006), pp. 166-168.

degree. At the University of London in 1919 he presided at the inauguration of the Chair of Russian. His knighthood in 1917 was partly in recognition of these services. Profoundly patriotic, Vinogradoff was thoroughly demoralized by the defeat of Russia and the triumph of Bolshevism and "Red Terror", suffering irreparable spiritual pain when he renounced his Russian citizenship in 1918. His material circumstances were adversely affected by the Russian Revolution, and rapidly failing eyesight compounded his difficulties.

During the second half of 1923 Vinogradoff returned to the United States together with his wife, addressing the Institute of Politics at Williamstown and thoroughly denouncing the Soviet regime. The autumn and winter were spent at the University of California at Berkeley, and then by offering courses at the Universities of Michigan, Columbia, Yale, and Johns Hopkins.

Contemporaries described Vinogradoff as "neo-Kantian" in his juristic views, strongly individualistic but, typically Russian, aware of the social individual as well. As a teacher he was inspired and inspiring, but not easy for the ordinary University undergraduate to comprehend. Fisher said that to the bright and advanced he was a fountain of methodological rigor and knowledge. Demanding to the point of being severe, his standards of meticulous scholarship were unsympathetic to the indolent or the careless. He himself worked formidable hours, endowed with a strong constitution and powers of concentration, often working twelve-hour days for sustained periods in succession. Before events in Russia led him to seek intellectual refuge in constructs of the mind, he was a sociable conversationalist, fond of music (he was a considerable pianist thanks to his mother) and the arts, above all the theatre. Chess was his favorite relaxation, and he played with better than average proficiency. Endowed with a quick, satirical sense of humor, he was beneath his magisterial demeanor amiable and shrewdly perceptive, a man of courage, powers of decision, and a considerable obstinacy once his mind was set on what he deemed to be right and wise.

Fisher further observed that there was a close link between his lectures and his books, the lectures being constantly revised and reworked before deemed to be ready for publication. A voracious reader, he integrated his perceptions and reactions into as many as five revisions of his typescripts, calling readily upon his memory for citations and references.

As noted above, the *Encyclopedia Britannica* later called Vinogradoff "perhaps the greatest authority of his day on feudal law and customs of England". And this assessment is a just one. Having begun as a social historian, Vinogradoff from the very outset began to devote special attention to legal institutes. He himself explained his turn towards legal research as follows:

> ... [T]he law regulating social conditions is not merely an external superstructure, but as to social facts it is both an influence and a consequence. In one sense it is a most valuable product of the forces at play in the history of society, most valuable just by reason of the requirements of its formalism and of those theoretical tendencies which give a very definite even if a somewhat distorted shape to the social processes which come within its sphere of action ... There is no law, however subtle and comprehensive, which does not exhibit on its logical surface seams and scars, testifying to the incomplete fusing together of doctrines that cannot be brought under the cover of one principle. And so a dialectic examination of legal forms which makes manifest the contradictions and confused notions they contain actually helps us to an insight into the historical stratification of ideas and facts, a stratification which cannot be abolished however much lawyers may crave for unity and logic.[16]

In studying the period of English history from Henry II to Edward I, Vinogradoff concluded: "Indeed one of the best means that we have for estimating the social process of those times is afforded by the formation and the break up of legal notions in their cross influences with surrounding political and economic facts.

---

16. P. G. Vinogradoff, *Villainage in England. Essays in English Mediaeval History* (1892), pp. 127-128.

Vinogradoff considered the history of law to be an integral part of social history, its most important aspect.[17] This attention to the legal aspect of the historical process enabled him to refute or clarify a series of conceptions held by English historians who specialized in the social system of England during the Middle Ages. Vinogradoff in particular established that the "system of estates depicted by the ancient jurists of the Saxons was based on the predominant significance of the free people, and not on the domination of the aristocracy", that "in the tenth and eleventh centuries society was reordered on feudal principles" and that nonetheless certain categories of the population who were dependent upon land retained their personal freedom, and that folkland is the "most ancient form of land possession, limited by the right of ancestry and confirmed not by an act, but by folk customs and certification".

On the other hand, studies of social relations enabled Vinogradoff to show how English jurists of the thirteenth century were excessively speculative and divorced from practical life in constructing villainage in terms of Roman slavery. The theories of English legal writers of the thirteenth century, Vinogradoff noted, were incompatible with a series of facts "characterizing the position of the villain as such which could not be drawn from a single principle, either from slavery or from freedom, or from colonus, but included elements of each of those three conditions and therefore must be explained only historically". The "study of the legal aspect of villainage discovers three elements in its complex structure. Legal theory and political arbitrariness are ready to make it almost slavery; the manorial system ensures a status for it somewhat similar to the Roman colonus; in addition, there exists an element of freedom in it which speaks of the Saxon tradition".

Being an historian of social relations, Vinogradoff looked upon the essence of law in a special way. He criticized the definition of law accepted in his day as the aggregate of the rules of behavior

---

17. Vinogradoff, *English Society in the Eleventh Century* (1908), p. 12.

established and enforced by a sovereign power, that is, the State. Historically, this definition emanated, he pointed out, from Thomas Hobbes (1588-1679) as adapted by John Austin (1790-1859), and through him by the majority of English jurists. In his words "this theory approaches law purely in its formal aspect. It does not allow any research of legal norms from the standpoint of their internal content and does not consider the character of that political power which is the supreme authority in the State at all. Law for it is a receptacle which one may fill with any liquid. A harsh, unjust norm is as lawful as the most just law". The weakness of the positivist doctrine of law Vinogradoff considered to be its unacceptability for canon law, international law, and other legal systems not linked directly with State power. "The truth is obviously that not unilateral prescription, but agreement, serves as the basis of law", Vinogradoff wrote.

The substantiation of the definition of a legal norm as prescription Vinogradoff linked especially with the fact that it does not provide an answer as to whether a law is binding only upon those who receive the prescription, or also upon those who issue it. "If the essence of law is coercion, then the law is binding only upon subjects and subordinates; higher persons of State are above or outside it", he noted.

In Vinogradoff's words, the element of coercion in law, although it is present,

> nonetheless is not an absolutely essential indicia of a legal norm. We can look upon it as the most convenient means of coercing the performance of a law, but we cannot regard it as the essence of legal relations. It is evident that one should add coercion based on personal acknowledgement and public opinion ... The law has the purpose to effectuate rights and justices, although in individual instances it perhaps achieves this aim rather imperfectly ... A certain equilibrium must exist in every system of law between justness and power. And it follows that a definition of law may not be based exclusively on a concept of State coercion.

Vinogradoff drew special attention when eliciting the essence of law not to the means, but to the end. He was not satisfied by the Kantian theory which saw the ultimate purpose of law in freedom, and the principal function as harmonizing the freedom of one person with the freedom of other members of society. In Vinogradoff's view,

> the concept of freedom here is not properly drawn, for it is evident that the agreement reached by law inevitably must consist of reducing individual freedom, and freedom in its ordinary understanding only opens the possibility for activity but does not specify the direction of this activity.

Vinogradoff also did not agree with Rudolf von Jhering (1818-1892), so popular in his day amongst Russian jurists; Jhering regarded the purpose of law as delimiting interests. Vinogradoff wrote:

> in making the State the supreme judge over conflicting interests, Jhering assumed a grave duty. Neither the State nor laws can assume an impossible task -- to subordinate to their influence all interests which arise in social life and to direct individual persons in the selection and realization of these interests.

Vinogradoff's final conclusion with regard to the problem of the essence of law was: "We can therefore say that the purpose of law is the regulation of the distribution and realization of human might over persons and things in the process of social communion". In accordance with this understanding of law, Vinogradoff defined law as a "number of rules relative to the distribution and realization of might over persons and things -- rules which have been established and the performance of which is required by society". In his view the definition of law offered by him is appropriate to all stages of historical development.

> It is as correct with respect to primeval legal norms, the performance of which is enforced to a significant degree by coercion, but also with respect to those highly-complex State organizations

of the present day which endeavor to create perfected systems of judicial means of the defense of rights and State sanctions. It embraces both municipal decrees, customs, and degrees of autonomous organizations, and the common law and parliamentary legislation. The binding force of constitutional and international law find their place within it. It takes into account criminal and civil law, punishment, and the sanction of nullity. Its principal virtue is that it accords greater significance to the purpose of law than to the means by which enforcement is sought.

Vinogradoff attached enormous significance to law in the life of human society. "Law", he wrote, "may not be reconciled with the dominance of factual conditions which too often reflect force and exploitation. It aspired to more than to merely what is -- to that which should be. Despite all of the inadequacies and shortcomings, there is a moral greatness in it". Vinogradoff was a proponent of the rule-of-law State. "Law", he believed, "is the foundation of a healthy State life". It is "not in power, but in law, and to some extent in the State itself for which it exists, that law is proclaimed and implemented".

His major work on historical jurisprudence remained uncompleted. Intended to be a number of volumes, it promised a new theory of law based on the identification of various historical types of law. The two volumes which appeared were awarded the Swiney Prize, offered every fifth year "for the best published work in Jurisprudence". As a comparatist who painted with a very broad brush,[18] he was nonetheless acutely aware of the limitations and dangers of the comparative method unskillfully used. It is not, he said, "the juxtaposition of resembling facts but the dialectical examination of given principles in various surroundings which yields fruitful and somewhat unexpected results".

Vinogradoff was a remarkable bridge between England and Russia, without precedent in the field of law. He remains apparently

---

18. See T. I. Schechter, "Paul Vinogradoff – the Pontiff of Comparative Jurisprudence", *Illinois Law Review*, XXIV (1929-30), pp. 528-546.

the only legal scholar to have been a member of both the British and Russian Academies and was the only Russian scholar to have been knighted by the British Crown. A portrait of Sir Paul Vinogradoff by Henry Lamb was presented to him at a dinner held in All Souls College, Oxford, on 13 June 1925. Originally it hung in the Maitland Library in the Examination Schools at Oxford and presently in the Bodleian Library. A lithograph of the portrait, signed by Sir Paul, was presented on 1 May 1997 by the Vinogradoff family to The Vingradoff Institute, with whom it remains.[19]

---

19. Sir Paul said of the portrait: "I do not think that it is a flattering likeness, but I like it better for that, for it will show to our successors the earnest and somewhat sad face and the meditative look of one who has marveled at many riddles in this world without being able to solve them". Quoted in Fisher, note 12 above, pp. 68-69.

INTERNATIONAL ORGANIZATION

THE LEGAL AND THE POLITICAL ASPECTS OF THE LEAGUE OF NATIONS

[Originally published in *The Russian Commonwealth*,
no. 1 (1 November 1918, pp. 5-9]

A great deal of the uncertainty and skepticism concerning a League of Nations is produced by confusion between the legal and the political aims of such a League. It is supposed by many that the acceptance of the idea is bound to lead to a complete upheaval in Constitutional as well as in International Law; to the substitution of vague internationalism for the historical organization of States; to the abolition of national armies and fleets for the sake of a cosmopolitan armed force; to indiscriminate interference in the affairs of every single commonwealth; in fact, to a kind of world Socialism run by International Boards. In the view of others, although such a revolution may not be in sight just now, there is a great danger that the acceptance of the principle of international control, even in its moderate form, may prove the thin edge of the wedge in the gradual destruction of the system of national States with which the progress of European civilization has hitherto been intimately connected. Sometimes again, the treatment of State conflicts on judicial lines, incautious promoters of the League may jeopardise the success of more modest and yet highly desirable schemes, for which the way has been opened by the great crisis of the world war.

It seems to us that a firm and precise formulation of the two-fold nature of the prospective League may remove many misgivings. The misery and degradation of Armageddon have made everyone realize that things cannot go on in the old grooves of crafty diplomacy, ruthless violence, and hypocritical selfishness, tempered only by the necessity of making preparations for successful onslaughts. The abominable traditions of statecraft bequeathed by Frederick II, by Napoleon, by Metternich, and by Bismarck, must be reversed. The fact that an overwhelming Alliance of leading Powers has been formed in order to assert right against violence, makes such a reversal possible and necessary. The best guarantee of success in this momentous undertaking is to be sought not in the weakening of the material forces of this Alliance, but in directing these forces towards aims of justice and progress. A long time will pass before disarmament on a large scale can be carried out. Even after peace and demobilisation the great champions of Humanity – Great Britain, the United States, France – will have to keep their "shining armour" bright in order to safeguard the results obtained, and to provide the nucleus of force without which a League of nations would be a mere fiction liable to be exploded by an unscrupulous and resolute malcontent. We cannot afford to dilute national organisations: we have to start from them and to combine them for common purposes.

I.

These purposes are obviously of two kinds. It is not since yesterday that civilized mankind has recognised the necessity of submitting relations between States to the operation of laws. As a consequence of the world war in the XVIIth century – the Thirty Years' War – a body of usages and conventions has grown up as the basis of substantive International Law, and we have witnessed in our time many attempts, particularly at the Hague Conferences, to codify important sections of this law. The weak side of all these attempts has been the absence of adequate sanction – the dependence of all arrangements on the good faith of the Powers concerned. Sturdy burglars have broken the most emphatic rules over and over again, and there has never been a tribunal competent to call them to justice, or a force capable of coercing them, not by self-help, but by the execution of a sentence. The XXth century world struggle must lead to the completion of the work of the XVIIth. International Law has to be provided with effective sanction, and this is the first task a League of Nations has to set itself. It is not a Utopia to desire that such acts as the Aerenthal annexation of Bosnia and Herzegovina, or the violation of Belgium's neutrality by one of the guarantors, should be proceeded against by judicial methods, and that the sentence pronounced on the culprit should be carried out by the united forces of the League, or by a combination of its best armed members. As a matter of fact, if the authority of the League were substituted for the uncertain threat of reprisals by chance coalitions, neither of these two outrages would have taken place. Such master strokes of Machiavelian rapacity have been rendered possible by the anarchical condition of the world.

It is evident also that whether the League of Nations is already constituted or not, it is to some judicial authority that numberless infringements of the International Law in the course of the present war will have to be referred: the sinking of ships at sight, attacks on hospital ships, the inhuman treatment of prisoners, atrocities in the field, the wanton destruction of towns, etc., etc. call for retribution. In spite of the pronouncement of a high juridical authority, it seems to us that it is on this legal and judicial side that the possibilities of the League of Nations are especially clear and plain.

(*a*) This is recognised in most projects by the institution of a *Court* for the settlement of all disputes arising out of the infringement of express International rules or of conventions between States.

It would be useless to discuss in detail the modes of elaboration of such rules. The projects have generally in view a *Conference* or *Congress* of the members of the League in which this matter would be referred, and in dealing with the *Constitution* of the League its framers will have to consider questions as to membership, majority (simple and qualified), ratification, etc. How far the Congress will accept pre-existing laws, such as the Geneva, of the Hague Conventions, and to what extent new ground must be reclaimed, it will have to decide for itself. Our present object is merely to point out that it is the first duty of the League of Nations to provide for such a combination of legislative, judicial, and executive machinery as to render international rules as effective in their application as the rules of Constitutional or Private Law.

(*b*) The enforcement of *Conventions* appears as the second clearly established duty of the *Court*. There are countless occasions when States enter into agreements among themselves as to commercial relations, loans, exploitation of mines, forests, fisheries, etc., literary copyright, the use of watercourses, railway, telegraph lines, etc. Disputes arising as to the interpretation or the actual working of these conventions may be referred in the first instance to arbitrators in accordance with existing practice, but the Court of the League ought to act even in such cases as a Court of Error (Cour de Cassation), and in some specified instances as a Court of Appeal, while reserving to itself original jurisdiction in matters of common interest – for instance, as regards postal union.

(*c*) There is no complete agreement in the projects as to a third class of cases, namely as to claims of individuals against States and of States against individuals. It is difficult to see, however, why private individuals or corporations, aggrieved by the action of a State, should be debarred from claiming redress through the Court of the League. In many cases such individuals or corporations may prefer acting through the State to which they belong, but this must be left to their own discretion. There is no juridical reason why, for instance, a banking concern that has negotiated a loan for a foreign Government should be prevented from suing the debtor before the Court of the League. The Venezuela conflict would have followed a different course if it had been conducted on such lines. But, certainly, precautions must be taken against futile suits, and some sort of committee for a preliminary sifting of claims will have to be instituted, while a special section of the Court may be set down for dealing with cases under private International Law in so far as the League takes cognisance of them.

(*d*) A fourth class of cases may arise if States or individuals (and corporations) approach the Court with claims based, not on codified rules or conventions, but on general principles of justice. In the present inchoate stage of International Law, such an eventuality is bound to arise frequently. It is evident, for instance, that the new technical processes which are being discovered every day may result in situations which it would be impossible to bring within the range of express rules or conventions. The use of submarines and of aircraft have produced many vexed questions of this kind. In other cases the right claimed may be derived from general notions of justice; cases of wanton oppression by powerful States falling short of formal infringement of legal rules ought to be amenable to judicial decision on such lines (*e.g.*, the case of Serbia in 1914). Is the Court to refuse jurisdiction in such cases until the Conference (or Congress) has devised general rules on these matters? Such a course would be more than pedantic. It would deprive the new organisation of a great deal of its practical usefulness and authority. It seems reasonable to expect, that the Court may have recourse in such cases not only to logical extensions of principles recognised by existing rules, but to considerations of *equity*. Decisions of such lines may eventually result in the formation of a body of leading principles similar to the rules of Common law, or to the jurisprudential doctrines of the French Conseil d'Etat.

II.

The *political aspect* of the League of Nations presents much more difficult problems. The movement of opinion towards the constitution of International authority is by no means restricted to a settlement of conflicts which can be brought under the operation of juridical tests. Civilised mankind wants not merely to prevent gross breaches of *right*, but to establish some machinery for the conciliation of diverging *interests*, and for preventing crying abuses in the moral and social order. How would a League of Nations approach cases like the systematic misgovernment and the massacres of Turkey or the atrocities of white rulers in Africa and South America? International Law cannot be applied to such cases, and yet even under the old anarchical regime they excited indignation, and sometimes called forth remonstrances and impotent interference on the part of the Powes (Constantinople Conference of 1876, intervention in Crete, the Inspectorates in Macedonia, etc.). It is certainly desirable to establish a central clearing house for the arrangement of the innumerable cases of friction that will be inevitably produced even after the most fair and reasonable readjustment of right and power at the conclusion of the present war. Let us just think of the fermentation produced by the claims of nationalities, and the necessity of balancing these claims against the historical and geographical requirements of existing State organisations, of the aspirations of savage and half barbaric peoples towards self-government. Let us think also of the internal catastrophes connected with socialistic developments, of the possibility of Bolshevik pogroms, and of white terror repressions. A League of Nations cannot remain a passive spectator of such disturbances. At the same time, they cannot be treated by the methods of a tribunal, because they arise from the conflict of *interests* which have not assumed the form of *rights*, and which in many cases can hardly be brought within the compass of a legal system.

This is why both the principal projects submitted for public consideration (the British and the American one) contemplate the formation of a *Council* by the side of a Court. This institution is styled a Council of *Conciliation*, and this term indicates by itself that what is intended is pressure rather than compulsion. If persuasion and pressure can be brought to bear with effect, all the better. But one must not lose sight of cases of obstinacy or evasion. Measures to be taken in such cases may assume one of three forms:

(*a*) The League may leave the matter to follow its course, as a *conflict between sovereign States*, even to the extent of war. Even in such cases it must "keep the ring," not only in the sense of insisting on the observance of the received rules of war, but also by restricting the action of belligerents. An obligatory "moratorium" of six months has been suggested as a preliminary to hostilities, and such a requirement would go far to remove the danger of rash actions. In view of obvious military objections the term might, perhaps, be shortened to four or three months.

(*b*) The Council of the League ought to initiate discussions and to promote a prospective settlement of topics likely to cause trouble. In some cases such negotiations would lead to conventions elaborated by the Congress and submitted for confirmation by a qualified majority of the members – say, two-thirds. Precedents for settlements of that kind may be found in the Anti-slavery Resolutions of the early XIXth century, or in the Declaration of Berlin as to territorial claims in Africa. The advantage of such a process lies in the fact that in most cases Powers taking part in prospective discussions would find it difficult to contest principles, while they would oppose a rival power bringing forward an occasional claim in a similar direction. Once the stage of a general convention has been reached under the authority of the League, it will provide a basis for judicial action, and preclude subsequent conflicts between single States. It may be added that such a procedure should provide the line of least resistance in the matter of a limitation of armaments.

(*c*) In extreme cases the League may be obliged to interfere directly against disturbers of the peace, oppressors and pirates, even across the ordinary boundaries of State Sovereignty. The history of the XIXth century has been a number of such interventions in the cause of humanity and civilisation, and the recent intervention of the Entente Powers in Russia may be classed under this head. This is, undoubtedly, the most delicate point in the whole programme, but it has to be faced in the hope that the Council and the Congress of a League of Nations, led by the great Democratic Powers – Great Britain, France and the United States – may prove worthy of a great trust imposed on it in the matter. It will have to undertake a task similar to that which the Holy Alliance set to itself, but to carry it out in an exactly opposite direction, for the sake of freedom, enlightenment and justice.

THE REALITIES OF A
LEAGUE OF NATIONS

[Published for the first time.* Typewritten manuscript with emendations in Vinogradoff's hand which have been incorporated here. HLSL SC MD, Vinogradoff Papers, Box 7, folder 10. The Finding Aid and the relevant folder erroneously attribute this manuscript to a Letter to The Times, published as "The Covenant of the League" on 28 March 1919 (see below). On two occasions in the manuscript Vinogradoff has introduced a typewritten cross-reference indicating the passages were to be inserted from his article in *Russian Commonwealth* published in 1 November 1918. The manuscript is undated but would be after 1 November 1918 and possibly early in 1919 – WEB]

[I]

The catastrophe of the War has brought home to all thinking men that fact that we are not only spectators but actors in the greatest crisis in history. Empires have been thrown into the melting pot, and the future depends on how far in their transformed shapes the States of the world will prove more solid and satisfactory than their predecessors. One of the most inspiring ideas arising from this mighty upheaval is the conviction that civilised mankind is bound to prevent a recurrence of barbaric struggles in which millions of the best and noblest are sacrificed and the welfare of generations are destroyed for the sake of futile agrandisements and imaginary prestige. The heroic deeds of the Allies have prevented the worst: they have warded off the menace of universal enslavement, but the fruits of victory achieved at a tremendous cost must not be squandered in apathy and thoughtlessness. As [an] "overwhelming" combination of the Entente has been able to put out the fire by mighty efforts, it ought to be able by foresight and watchfulness to prevent its breaking out again. The Entente should develop into a League of

---

* Published with permission. "The Realities of a League of Nations" [ca. 1919], Sir Paul Vinogradoff Papers, Harvard Law School Library, Box 7, Folder 10.

Nations to keep pace and to ensure justice. It is a difficult problem, but the progress of political thought and the circumstances of the time provide such materials and such opportunities as have never existed before. Our generation would be guilty of an unforgivable offence if it did not make full use of the opportunity presented by the smelting process of the world's crucible.

In order to achieve good results in this attempt, it is especially important to notice the principal obstacles and to steer towards definite aims. To my mind the greatest danger ahead does not lie in the traditional scepticism as to a possible settlement of international conflicts, but in the confusing wealth of ideas dominating our time and competing for supremacy in our attention and activities. There are three [four] great ideas let loose, as it were, in the domain of political organisation: 1) the striving of nationalities towards self-determination, 2) the self-consciousness of the historical States, proud of their past and hopeful of the future, 3) the claim of labour to an adequate place in political and social life, 4) the ideal of international justice. Each of these great ideas would be sufficient in itself to absorb the entire energy of civilised mankind in the course of an epoch. As it happens, they are all active at the same time and although in truth they ought to supplement each other, in practice they not only overlap, but complete and limit one another. It is evident, for example, that it would be out of the question to dissolve the traditional organisms of civilised Empires like Great Britain in order to satisfy to the full the possible claims of all nationalities included in them. In various degrees the historical State combinations will have to be balanced and compromised in some way with the tendency towards self-determination: and this imposes on the prospective League one material limitation. It cannot be composed of all the Nations on the face of the earth but of Nations fir [sic: fit] to be embodied in self-sufficient State organisations. It will be a League of States compatible as far as possible with the wide exercise of National rights. Fancy for one moment Great Britain broken up into its national elements, Ireland, Wales, and Scotland pulling each its own way, not so speak of the innumerable races of backward and alien civilisation.

On the other hand – as the foundations of our States have to be strengthened by appeals to racial psychology and national unity, our aspirations towards international justice must assume a specific form. There can be no question, at this stage at any rate, of giving up the distinctions of separate States and welding them into an International Commonwealth. People feel keenly that they are British, French, Americans, Russians, Serbs before being citizens of the world. This being so, the new order must be built up as a League and not as a Federal Government, conceding a certain amount of autonomy to its component parts but towering over all its members and ready to compel them in the most important matters even against their will. Again, one of the most powerful currents making for international order is undoubtedly the striving of the working classes to get rid of anarchical competition in economic matters. The disputes between Capital and labour do not concern us in this connection in so far as they are restricted to conflicts in a given society, but Capital is international in its essence and the interdependence of the various countries as parts of the world's economic organism is so great that it is out of the question to treat questions of supply and demands of work and wages of the basis of local conditions. The leaders of the Labour movement are therefore naturally led to demand regulations as to the distribution of material, as to wages, sanitary legislation, standards of life which should stretch over the boundaries of existing States and involve international government in economic matters. But, to mention only one or two difficult points, how are we to reduce to equal or even to approximately proportional standards the requirements of British, German, Russian and Chinese working men. No amount of legislation, supervision and compulsion can abolish differences produced by centuries of national growth. Similarly I fail to see by what means wages can be regulated on international lines. Altogether, the leaders of the League of Nations will have to take good care that their patronage of producers and middlemen should not degenerate into bureaucratic despotism.

There is no harm in limitations when it is fully understood that common action for peace and justice will rest in this case not so much on a rigid constitution, but on the free resolve of the members to ward off bloodshed and encroachments. It would not only be unpracticable – it would be harmful to raise a Federal Government over the whole world, and to charge it with the final direction of all difficult affairs and all conflicting tendencies of mankind. No one government could master such a task, no human beings could assume such a responsibility. As has been well said in one of the papers published by the "Round Table" on the subject: the scaffolding of the League of Nations would collapse if too great a burden should be piled up on it by incautious builders. And yet, the time has come and the means are at hand to combine the police of the leading civilised nations in such a way as to avoid general conflagrations and p[r]ovide channels for the peaceable adjustment of difficulties.

In order to achieve this result two main principles should be set up and applied with consistency: international law must cease to be the plaything of unscrupulous potentates, and political relations between States should be guided by the same fundamental requirements of honesty, common sense, conciliation as are usual in the intercourse between private persons. Institutions and forces are wanted in order that these two precepts may be carried into practice, and not rank as pious wishes, flimsy ornaments for speeches which are made one day and thrown to the winds the next day.

II.

The creation of a real international law stands in need of one main contrivance. The rules of this law must be provided with adequate sanctions, that is with the guarantees of their enforcement. In themselves the rules of the Geneva Convention, of the Hague Conventions, of the Declaration of Paris are carefully formulated and generally recognised laws. Their drawback hitherto has been the absence of a tribunal for trying offenders against these rules and of an executive for punishing lawbreakers. The solemn declaration that Belgium is a neutral country was complete as a statement of right, but it had no regular sanction behind it and therefore one of the powers that had agreed to maintain it consigned it to the waste paper basket with no other risk but that of a fight with some chance protector of the victim. Such a state of things will not be tolerated any longer when the League makes up its mind to call law-breaking States to the bar of a real tribunal and forces them to stand by their engagements, to compensate damages, or to incur some specific penalty. The creation of a Court with high authority in matters of International Law and the firm resolve of the League to enforce the decisions of this Court is the first measure required in order to give reality to the ideal of a League of Nations. This would constitute an immense stride in the progress of mankind. Ever since the XVIIIth. Century when the calamities of the Thirty Years War called forth the first systematic attempts of international jurisprudence, ever since the age of Grotius, jurists and statesmen have been seeking in vain the road towards sanctioned and safeguarded international justice. It has been reserved for our time to clear the way towards the solution of the problem.

III.

But this is not enough. On many occasions bitter hostility between Nations and States has arisen in consequence, not of infringed rights, but of conflicting interests. We read every day of bitter controversies between Czechs and Germans, Poles and Ukrainians, Russians and Turks, Bulgarians and Serbians, Italians and Yugoslavs: many of these controversies spring from conflicting claims of nationalities as to territory; others are derived from economic competition; others may have a background of religion and cultural antipathies. In the old days these antagonisms would have resolved themselves in sanguinary wars and endless fluctuations of so-called victories and very real defeats. With the coming into existence of a League of Nations the immense weight of an organised public opinion of mankind ought to act as a salutary influence for pacification, making all these quarrels shrink in their pettiness and setting against them the common sense and equity of universal civilisation. There will be at the disposal of the League many material means for bringing adversaries to reason: they may be compelled to resort to arbitration; they may be prevented from taking hasty action by the imposition of an enforced term for reflection and negociation; they may be subjected to measures of economic isolation. At the same time it must be admitted that the League cannot assume responsibility for a final settlement of all disputes in which an opposition of interests is at stake, as distinct from an infringement of rights. Take an instance: there is a strong view in the American West and in the Australian Commonwealth that the immigration of Chinese and Japanese should be prevented: the people of California and Australia want to build up their commonwealths on the solid basis of settlement by the White race. There is strong feeling among the Japanese and Chinese, on the other hand, that discrimination against them in this matter is offensive and unjustifiable, and there are weighty material reasons why the leading States of the "Yellow race" press for expansion by emigration. The League of Nations will certainly do all it can to mitigate the sharpness of the conflict and to pave the way for a compromise, but could it take upon itself to decide between the two contentions and to compel the Australians to admit certain foreign settlers, or to compel the Japanese to abstain from seeking admission to the Pacific Continent? Evidently note, unless the League is prepared to take over the Government of the world. At the same time it is clear that even in such a case of irreconcilable conflict the advent of the League will mark a complete change from past methods of dealing with such matters. Instead of sharpening weapons for an armed conflict which might break out at any moment, the contending parties will probably be driven to a deadlock as long as a suitable compromise has not been discovered and no act of one-sided violence can be attempted in the meantime. In such positions the negative solution, the side which says no to a claim, has the formal advantage, but substantial considerations of expediency are sure to make themselves felt in time in the sense of some give and take arrangement.

 It is not absolutely excluded that some of these conflicts of interests, when envenomed by racial and cultural antagonism, may burse into actual hostilities in spite of all the restraining influences brought to bear on the adversaries by the League. It would be premature to hope that South American republics or Asiatic border

States would be prevailed upon to turn swords into ploughshares once for all, or that International police should be always ready at hand. To judge by what is happening just now in Eastern Europe in front of the "overwhelming" hosts of the Entente, there may be objections to police action of the League on the part not only of the culprit but also of the police powers. Such isolated feuds would be of minor importance and short duration, however, and could not in any way be compared with the gigantic struggles and the exhausting preparations so characteristic of the conditions which we have witnesses up to now. We have been assured by authoritative representatives of the three leading States of the Entente, that certain fundamental conditions are bound to prevent these States from merging their interests in those of an International Confederation in the absolute manner demanded by abstract doctrine. France cannot disarm on land while she is confronted by an ambitious and unscrupulous nation which, though vanquished at present, may think of Revanche and disposes of a population almost twice as large as that of France itself. Great Britain cannot disarm on sea, because her existence and the connection of her parts depends on her naval superiority. The United States has no thought of entangling herself in the conflicts and alliances of European powers, tending to keep up the material superiority of some of them over others. It is true that President Wilson and his numerous followers stand up energetically for a League of all peoples, but it is easier to set up the ideal of such a League than to mould the world in accordance with its principles. The disorder, the disasters, the crimes produced by the present state of fermentation stink in our nostrils, and yet the adepts of the new order are spending more time in pageants and rejoicings than in the pacification of the troubled world. It is a familiar saying that we do not want to embark on new wars, a sequel to old ones, that our soldiers are tired and long to be home. But it is certainly not a suitable expression of the spirit of international government. It may be a hard task, but it is only by the wise and firm treatment of present problems in their extreme and distressing forms that a measure will be set to the practical value of any scheme of international improvement. It is the stern duty of our age to see the work begun by the great struggle against German militarism carried out to its ultimate consequences, even if this should involve further sacrifices and hardships. It is necessary for the fulfilment of the task that it should be reduced to its essential features.

It seems almost as if the historical process by which an end was put to private wars in the Middle Ages were going to repeat itself in the case of the Public wars of modern times. Europe about the year 1000 A.D. was a cockpit in which every baron and every fortified town was constantly at war with neighbouring barons and towns. The Church was the first to preach peace and to introduce a kind of "international law". The prelates began by trying unsuccessfully to bind belligerents over and to keep complete peace. This absolute renouncement could not be carried out, and many of those who made the most solemn vows were the first to break them. Subsequently partial restrictions were imposed and they proved effective and practical: people could not fight in churches or in churchyards; they could not fight during holidays and week-days, week-ends too from Thursday to Monday. In this way the ground was prepared for the rising State authorities to step in and to stamp out private war – in favour of a State monopoly. Let us hope to see the beginning of effective measures for stamping out these State monopolies for the sake of a World League. But it would be a fatal mistake to assume that the world is ready for an immediate and permanent settlement on the lines of international government. The stage of the League of Nations must be passed first, and it will require some time before its tasks and possibilities have been exhausted.

IV.

As we cannot renounce States built up on national and territorial lines another perplexing problem will have to be faced. To what extent is misgovernment and oppression to be tolerated within the precincts of these single States? It is all very well to concede independent sovereignty to commonwealths in the management of their home affairs, but there were moral limits to non- the Greeks in the early years of the XIXth century; not only enthusiastic Philhellenes like Lord Byron, but the governments of England and France, and even the champion of the Holy Alliance, Emperor Nicholas, took up arms and came to the rescue of the Sultan's Greek subjects. When the Bulgarians were being massacred in the seventies indignation spread over Europe and a war of liberation was waged by Russia. In consequence of the Armenian and Macedonian massacres all sorts of lame expedients – inspectorates, conferences, and the like – were tried to keep the legitimate Sovereign within bounds. All the more – under the supervision of the League such extreme cases of misrule ought not be tolerated. A flagrant case of this kind, if I may be allowed to say so, is presented by Bolshevist tyranny in Russia, where the entire educated class – not very numerous at best – is threatened with extermination. We have thus to recognise the possibility and necessity of intervention in the affairs of Sovereign States on behalf of the organised public opinion of mankind as expressed by the League. Needless to say, however, that such intervention must be directed to the removal of crying abuses, and that it would be out of the question to start on a series of crusades in order to remedy all sorts of evils and errors. Such a policy would not only be impracticable, but it would lead to intolerable oppression and to boundless disaffection on the part of the nations subjected to such meddling. No hard and fast line can be drawn beforehand between wise and foolish measures in this respect. Everything, as in many other human affairs, will depend on discretion, tact and common sense. The Congresses and executive representatives of the League will undoubtedly have a vast scope for their deliberations and for the exercise of ability and character. The task will certainly be worthy of their well intentioned efforts.

It would be out of the question to attempt on the present occasion to outline however briefly the constitutional machinery with which the League should be provided. The problem of combining a proper self-determination of members with an efficient organisation of the whole is unquestionably beset with very great difficulties. I may just point out in passing the complex nature of any assessment of power, if I may use the expression, as to the relative weight of vote and influence between the various States, no different in size, strength, wealth and civilisation. The hold system of counting every international personality as a unit will not do in a League intended not to express pious wishes, but to frame decisions and to enforce their execution. Some kind of agreement as to voting power and the attribution of rights and duties will have to be arrived at by consent. The immense advantages to be derived from such an agreement will, let us hope, make it a reality. It is a firm prospect, in any case, that we can look forward to something else besides tending wounds, carrying out repairs and paying off loans. The war has not been fought in vain if it can be made the starting point of a new era in which the cynical principle of unrestricted selfishness in politics is discarded once and for ever, and the nations of the world choose as the guiding star of international intercourse the idea of *justice*.

THE COVENANT OF THE LEAGUE

GREAT AND SMALL POWERS

An International Aim

[*The Times*, 28 March 1919, p. 7]

To the Editor of The Times.

Sir, –

May I ask for some space in the columns of *The Times* in order to offer some suggestions as to the Covenant of the League of Nations elaborated by the Committee of the Peace Conference? The subject is of such immense importance, and the draft Covenant calls forth so many objections, that it is the duty of all those who approve of the main principles of a League to contribute, as far as possible, towards the removal of serious defects in the present scheme. It would be deplorable if the unique opportunity presented by the outcome of the war were squandered on attempts to construct a kind of Tower of Babel which it would be impossible to keep up without an unbearable strain on the resources and the harmonious cooperation of the Powers concerned. For my part, I should like to call attention to the following points: –

1. The formation of the Executive Council, as provided for by Article 3, lends itself to the objection that, as long as the "representatives" of minor States are nominated by five Great Powers, the Executive Council will give effect, not to the views of a League of Nations, but to the views of the victors. But even when the additional members are chosen by the Body of Delegates, they will certainly not "represent" that Body, consisting of so many heterogeneous elements; no formal selection of four deputies can do justice to the various interests and tendencies of the States grouped together in the so-called Body of Delegates. In what sense

would, say, Belgium, Sweden, Poland, and Brazil "represent" the interests of Norway, Czech-Slovakia, Russia, and China? Can any combination be devised by which States competing with each other can assume the representation of interests opposed to their own? And is the internationalism of the existing States strong enough to create a basis for common elections? Do not the fierce antagonisms between Poles and Ukrainians, between Hungarians and Romanians, between Italians and Southern States, serve as a warning in this respect? If it is recognized that minorities should be represented in home affairs, the necessity for giving expression to conflicting tendencies is even more obvious in international arrangements. It seems to me that the idea of creating a fictitious representation should be given up, and that the Body of Delegates should be able to formulate its views on executive problems in its own midst. This will lead sometimes to conflicts of opinion between the Body of Delegates and the Council, but such open conflicts will be less injurious to the common cause than perpetual discontent with a pretence at representation, which may be regarded as a device for ensuring the domination of certain Great Powers.

2. The difficulty as to the "unanimity" of decision in case of coercive measures (Article 15) arises from an unsatisfactory attempt to ensure the application of sanctions to all kinds of disputes. They can be applied automatically only in trials as to right decided by judicial process; in such cases the decisions to be enforced will proceed not from the Council, but from a Court of Justice, so that the question of unanimity between Powers will not arise at all. Submission to such decisions and execution of such decisions can be guaranteed in advance by special treaties. The case is entirely different when conflicts of political interests come before the Council of the Body of Delegates. In such cases neither the submission of the parties nor the execution by the League can be guaranteed prospectively and automatically. Conflicts of this kind must be treated on their merits by political agencies, and neither unanimity nor majority of votes can decide. The constitutional objection raised in the United States expresses in a drastic form the inherent difficulty of the subject. The real advantage to be derived from the League will consist in

the statesmanlike treatment of such disputes, and in the common resolve to prevent a recurrence of terrible catastrophes like the present one. It will be of immense importance to know that in a great emergency the mightiest nations, including the United States, are resolved to maintain general peace, even if it is impossible to guarantee in advance that all conflicts will be conducted to a final decision by a unanimous executive action of the Powers.

3. A third suggestion is connected with the second one. The obscurity and complexity of the present Covenant may be explained to some extent by the subordinate part assigned to the judicial factor (Articles 13 and 14). It is not enough to provide for a series of arbitrations; a High Court of international standing is necessary to develop the jurisdiction of the League on the basis of juridical experience. From its panel the Judges in various trials will have to be selected, but it is desirable that there should be continuity in the treatment of traditional equity and international law.

Yours Truly,

19, Linton Road, Oxford, March 27.   PAUL VINOGRADOFF

HISTORY OF THE
LAW OF NATIONS

HISTORICAL TYPES OF INTERNATIONAL LAW

Lecture Delivered at the
University of Leiden
by
SIR PAUL VINOGRADOFF, F.B.A.
Corpus Professor of Jurisprudence in the University of Oxford

I. HISTORICAL TYPES OF LAW

II. GREEK CITIES

III. THE JUS GENTIUM OF THE ROMANS

IV. THE WORLD STATE OF MEDIAEVAL CHRISTENDOM

V. THE INTERNATIONAL RELATIONS OF TERRITORIAL STATES

VI. MODERN DEVELOPMENTS

I. HISTORICAL TYPES OF LAW

Some 170 years ago a French judge, Montesquieu, published his famous book on the *Spirit of Laws*. His essay remains an imposing monument of eighteenth century literature, not because of its treatment of special questions, but because it calls attention to one of the greatest problems of social science. Apart from complicated doctrines, from rigid rules and professional details, laws have their spirit: and they aim at establishing order, at preventing and solving conflicts by peculiar methods. Taken as a whole they are as characteristic of a nation as its language or its literature.

Montesquieu not only formulated the problem, but also found an appropriate setting for it by showing that it depended to a great extent on the grouping of data on the lines of certain principal types of development. He sought the explanation of particular forms in the influence of the physical environment on the one side and in the tendencies of political organization on the other. He considered these physical influences, these political tendencies not only in their material aspects, but also in their reaction on what we now call social psychology: despotism must be supported by terroristic measures, the monarchical régime is bound up with notions of honour; republics live by the virtue of citizens.

Montesquieu was, however, the child of his time, he lacked historical perspective and was dominated by the influence of the pseudo-classical school; besides, he had not enough material to enable him to emancipate himself from his great predecessor and master, Aristotle. The experience of the old monarchy of France and of the parliamentary oligarchy of England did not suffice to enlarge in any fundamental way the setting given by the Greek philosopher. Montesquieu's book became a continuation of the *Politics* of Aristotle. Its title should have been not the "Spirit of Laws," but the "Spirit of Governments as expressed in their Laws." Such limitation would have been natural and quite justified. Aristotle was dealing with communities whose juridical life was concentrated in the activity of restricted circles of privileged citizens: the opposition between constitutional and private law could not make itself felt in the same way as in modern States. The main question was that of the attribution of power to the majority of the citizens, to a small number, or to one individual. It is from this point of view that Aristotle looked at the particular problems of justice, especially those of property and family relationship. Montesquieu, although confronted with a much more complex society, does not yet realise the decisive importance of the relations of private law; he is still concerned with the constitutional standpoint indicated by Aristotle, although he has to work with a modified classification of the forms of government. Without detracting from the well-merited fame of the *ancien régime* judge it may be said, I think, that his sketch of the Spirit of Laws remains on the surface of the juridical life of modern peoples.

When a century later Jhering became inspired by an analogous conception he treated the juridical institutions of Rome as a whole and gave the largest place to private law. But his *Spirit of Roman Law* remains an isolated monograph and when present day science tries to carry out Montesquieu's project it must reckon with other systems of law brought to the front by social evolution.

I beg you to note the term *system*: it is not used accidentally. The fact that the sum total of a more or less important and durable juridical situation gathers, so to speak, into a system of which the different parts tend to support and complete each other is more marked than is the case in other departments of thought. This is due to the fact that law in its professional elaboration and application always rests on operations of logic. Legislators formulate rules, judges apply them to particular cases and it would be absurd to issue conflicting rules or to apply them in a contradictory way: such cases occur in practice, but such actual inconsistencies are considered to be defects or flaws and juridical thought and jurisprudence tries to eliminate them as far as possible. The striving toward consistency and order is of the essence of juridical method, and the great creations of law present themselves in the form of systems. Let us observe that sometimes even the needs of practical life are sacrificed to this logical coherence. This is undoubtedly to be regretted, but from the point of view of social science this systematising tendency presents considerable advantages. We have to do in law not with detached and heterogeneous facts, but with combinations embracing different aspects of social intercourse and we are able in the course of an intelligent study to go back to fundamental conceptions.

This point once established, let us see how this interesting and difficult study of the spirit of law can be approached with the best chance of success. We can follow Aristotle's example, while enlarging the scope of the enquiry. Aristotle, and Montesquieu after him, have taken as the guiding principles of their work the forms of governmental organization. It is the constitution of public powers which provides them with a standpoint for observation in their comparative study of institutions. For us moderns these starting points are inadequate; we are compelled by all the experience of our social life to descend deeper, to take into account the organization of work as well the organization of power, the daily life of ordinary people even more than the actions of princes and legislators. This being so what distinguishing feature are we to select in arranging our data?

Now as the classifications of Aristotle and Montesquieu are inadequate because they start from the forms of State organization, it is natural to substitute for them a classification according to the forms of social organization. These forms, considered as types realised in the past or in the present, are not very numerous and permit of classification according to fairly simple distinguishing features. They are reducible so far to five principal types, each of which includes several varieties, while at the same time, intermediate and combined forms are produced by geographical and historical conditions. The five types which I have in view are the tribe, the city, the Church, the contractual association, the collectivistic organization. The tribe is a social type founded on relationship real or supposed, natural or artificial. This type, widespread among primitive societies, includes on the one hand peoples grouped according to the mystic marks of totemism, on the other, communities resulting from the extension of the natural family, matriarchal or patriarchal. Whatever may be the diversity of their institutions and customs, the law of these tribes affords a number of points of identity and analogy which are traceable to a common source, namely the idea of kinship.

The second type is furnished by the law of the city, of the circle or club of privileged citizens making use of their close cohesion to establish a more or less exclusive civil law. I need not remind you of the example of the Greek and Italian republics.

It is precisely in this field that Aristotle worked, and his writings are still the most instructive on the subject. And in spite of the great differences of temperament and conditions between the Greeks and the Romans, the idea of deducing their civil institutions from an identical source has often guided the learned: one work I will just mention — Fustel de Coulanges' *La Cité Antique*, which, except for the exaggerated influence attributed to ancestor worship, remains a remarkable monument of research as to the spirit of laws.

In the third place appears the no longer of citizens but of believers — the city of God projected upon the earth and looking for guidance to heaven — a type with an universal tendency, represented in different varieties by the Jewish nation, the canon law of Christendom, Mussulman law.

The fourth type is that formed by individualistic associations aiming at freedom of trade and opinion, the type represented particularly by our present day civilization, but embracing also the world of the Roman Empire. At first sight we are perhaps tempted to dispute the rightful claim of a class which should appeal to liberty and yet admit as one of its principal varieties the Rome of the despotic emperors. But a criticism of this kind seems based on a misunderstanding. It is not the form of government that is in question; but the general character of social intercourse, and there can be no doubt that the law set forth by the great jurisconsults of the first three centuries — Gaius, Papinian, Paul, Ulpian — is the most complete manifestation of free association among individuals. The fact that the public law of this system is centred round the absolute authority of the ruler is in itself a characteristic effect of atomistic individualism, it is an expression of the unlimited preponderance of a State indispensable in a society facing detached and variable wills. But of course such an inference is not obligatory and alongside of the imperial variety other combinations may be set up, such as those of modern democracies, appealing more or less to the idea of contract, which asserts itself even in public law.

Finally the outlines of a fifth type appear more and more clearly in our own day — a type of collectivist association which makes social solidarity the first consideration and is ready to sacrifice to a great extent the interests of individuals in order to escape from economic competition and the social subjection of the weak to the strong. It would be irrelevant to distinguish the varieties of this type — bureaucratic socialism, syndicalism, communism — what is obvious is that all the stages of this movement are marked by profound changes in law and that it is only on condition that the upholders of the new ideals succeed in elaborating a normal system of law that they will have achieved something durable in the history of civilization.

Let me notice in passing that the evolution of these groups is bound to assume some form of international intercourse, alliances and federations. For purposes of defence as well as for trade peoples in the most varied geographical surroundings and in entirely different ethnological combinations develop similar forms of self-help, arbitration, religious sanction. Thus in every stage of civilization we are met with characteristic features of international law.

It is clear that this classification does not aim at giving a full account of the local combinations which have come into existence in history; these combinations depend not only on ideas but also on the localities in which these ideas take form and on the cross currents coming from other systems. The theoratic tendency, for example, was necessarily realised in a different way in Jerusalem, in Rome in Baghdad; individualism has crystallised diversely in the countries of Latin and Anglo-Saxon civilisation. On the other hand, the same historical grouping passes successively in its evolution under the influence of different guiding ideas. In the history of Rome are displayed the applications of the trib principalle, of the city, and of imperial individualism. Mediaeval Europe is dominated in its law by an acknowledged dualism of which feudal isolation and ecclesiastical universality are the two poles. Our own time shows unquestionably the marks of a transitional period from an individualistic type to a compromise between individualism and collectivism. Thus the classification by social types does not claim to be a substitute for legal history, it is the first step towards historical jurisprudence, that is towards a study of the spirit of laws which aims at setting free a constituent element of prime importance — dialectics of social principles in law.

When an English judge refuses to uphold an agreement made restraint of trade, he carries out the consequences of the principle of individual liberty in economic relations. When the same English judge obeys the clause of the Trade Disputes Act of 1906 which forbids him to penalize a trade union whose agents have committed tortious acts in the course of a dispute between employees and employer, he submits to a rule suggested by a collectivist tendency. Leading ideas of this kind recur again and again in many variations like the themes in modern music, and it is certainly useful to be able to recognise them and to trace their developments and combinations.

Let us add that although observations of this kind allow us to reduce considerably the multiplicity of the phenomena of legal history, although the tendency to systematise may thus serve as a powerful instrument of generalisation, the governing ideas in question are not necessarily simple. They are all products of synthesis, although they are useful for juridical analysis. When we consider, for instance, the idea of the Church we have to form a conception into which enter mystical beliefs, moral sentiments, needs of social organization. The way in which these diverse elements are combined is not always the same and hence divergences arise in the very heart of the general type. The same can be said of other social ideas. It would be wrong to try to construct juridical systems attached to social types by abstract and absolute processes of reasoning. The study of historical reality is all the more attractive in that it makes the leading themes pass through all sorts of media and thereby discloses what is essential and what is accidental in the transformations of law.

In this quest for the spirit of laws we are certainly not animated by fatalistic resignation. As knowledge of the laws of nature does not deprive men of the possibility of turning them to profit, so the logical force of ideas does not condemn societies to go adrift under the sway of currents of opinion. These currents themselves are produced by the understanding and the will of men, and far-seeing guides, determined leaders, faithful workers are no less necessary in the onward social movement than are explorers, inventors, well-equipped craftsmen in the material world. The best vessel may be the victim of shipwreck, but it is the pride of free men to oppose danger by farsighted and stubborn efforts.

The peculiar attitude of historical reflection has been examined recently by Windelband and more fully by Rikkert. They lay stress on a profound opposition between the method of natural science and that of cultural science (*Naturwissenschaft* and *Kulturwissenschaft*); the former seeks for the invariable laws which govern the phenomena of nature and explain their constant recurrence: the latter is concerned with the manifestations of human activity in the work of civilization which never recur in the same form. The former studies the relations between causes and effects; the latter, the relations between ends and means; the former states; the latter values. There is obviously a great risk of exaggerating the parallelism of the two studies. It would be absurd for historians to abandon the enquiry into causes. However imperfect may be the methods of their 'miniature science' — to use Renan's expression — the scientific element in the research causes cannot be eliminated from any enquiry into the past, and statistics show clearly that human phenomena, in spite of all their disconcerting variety, may be reduced to recurring schemes. It is difficult to discern the dominant forces and to determine exactly their functions, but there can be no doubt of their existence, and the work of a historian, even when he is presenting literary descriptions, can never be dissociated from the relation of causes and effects, nor can he limit himself to observing the influences exerted by individuals on one another.

In spite of these criticisms as regards the argument of the cultural theory, it seems to emphasise rightly an essential element he historic method — namely the profound modification of scientific thought involved by the introduction of the idea of scientific thought involved by the introduction of the idea of value. Every effort of culture can and ought to be estimated according to standards which lie outside the causal relation in so far as they are bound up with the idea of the good: such are, instance, the conceptions of the preservation of the race, of the advance of the individual towards perfection, of the greatest welfare of the greatest number, of the salvation of the soul, of liberty, of social justice. In this way any history of civilization necessarily involves a selection and an appreciation of facts in relation to some ideal end. History is therefore subjective and idealistic in the sense that it estimates facts in accordance with their value for the realization of some ideal purpose.

In accepting such an orientation we do not wish to return to an idealistic monism similar to that preached by the school of Hegel. There is no question of applying to the natural or to the historical sciences a preconceived system claiming to discover in the phenomena of nature and of social life the manifestation of a world Spirit. This may be a beautiful vision, but is only a vision; it leads neither to science nor to scientific philosophy. The same must be said of the counterpart of this idealistic monism, the materialistic monism proclaimed by Marx, a disciple of Hegel. In his attempt at simplification, all forms human life are derived from one fundamental function, — production of goods for the needs of man. Public and private law, literature, science, philosophy, religion, in spite of their apparent independence, are regarded as mere superstructures imposed on the granite foundation of economics.

No divergence between the study of ideas and that of causes is admitted, because ideas and purposes appear only as consequences, and reality is governed by economic evolution. To what extent this movement which claims to be scientific is really visionary can be gathered, for example, from the fantastic assertions of the Marxists on the development of religious ideas. What is the Reformation, that great crisis which stirred the passions of European nations for centuries and which still divides them into distinct camps? For the Marxists it heralded simply the advent of the bourgeoisie disguised in a tissue of theological subtleties. What is Calvinism? "The religion of Calvin accorded with the tendencies of the boldest bourgeois spirits of his time. His doctrine of predestination was the religious embodiment of the fact that in the world of commercial competition success does not depend on a man's activity or personal gifts, but on circumstances over which he has no control". (Engels).

Speculations of this kind have nothing to do with the research of truth: they are evidently suggested by party fanaticism.

All the varieties of historic monism seem to be equally misleading, because they imply in one way or another the identity of fact and idea, of effect and end. Supposing for a moment that such an identity were at the basis of things in themselves, it would be quite impossible to demonstrate it scientifically because we are bound by the condition of our mind to consider everything that exists under two different aspects — the aspect of given facts and the aspect of their reaction on our receptive and active individuality. Philosophy may endeavour to reconcile these points of view, but scientific enquiry has to treat each series in accordance with the method appropriate to it.

This discussion of methods is not as remote from the announced subject of this lecture as it might seem at first sight. One of the principal manifestations of economic monism is the denial of the value of law. The fanatics of Marxism (e.g. Labriola) prophesy the disappearance of law in the new society delivered from the parasitism of capital.

It is useless to contest prophecies, but the observation of actual facts shows at every step the powerful influence of juridical ideas on the course of economic and social development.

In our own time it would be particularly difficult to disregard the legal guardianship exercised by the community in the regulation of contract of service and of the work of miners, or the provisions for sickness and old age. The positive influence of law makes itself felt more and more as we approach the rules of personal status, the relations between social groups, and finally, the rules of public law. Let me illustrate my meaning by calling attention to a familiar case — the regulation of succession. There is a marked contrast between the legal partition of property amongst heirs in French and Belgian law and the tendency towards the unification of landed property in English, Norwegian and, in some cases, German law. It is certainly not a simple effect of economic conditions, but also the manifestation of different legislative policies, the one working for small estates and the democratic distribution of fortunes, the other inspired by the desire to protect economic organizations against division and dispersal.

I mentioned 'legislative policies' but I ought rather to have said 'juridical tendencies', for it is not solely or even principally by direct legislation that the positive action of law is exercised. In the case under consideration, the partition of inheritances in French law was not simply decreed by the Code Napoleon: it was prepared long before by provincial custom. In the same way the Norwegian *odal* and the land settlements of English law came into existence in ancient times as results of popular habits. The causes of these divergences are many and should be studied by themselves, but what interests us at the moment are the tendencies towards certain social purposes which are expressed in these arrangements. Rules of intestate succession were hardly ever elaborated, voted on and promulgated by legislative assemblies: most sources of law, considered from the sociological point of view, are moulded by custom. Land law, family organization, succession and testament still bear many traces of the forms imprinted upon them by the practice of the Roman *paterfamilias* and of Germanic experts on legal lore. In England especially, the rules of Common Law are almost all connected with antecedents in historic life and with the practical equity of the Middle Ages. One thing is quite clear, and that is that outside the professional rules which occupy so large a place in our codes and statutes there lies a vast domain of non-legislative practice, worked out by those interested, irrespective of any dispute, for the every day conduct of business. When a man died in Old France, it was said "le mort saisit le vif", that is, the deceased passed on his rights to his natural heir in virtue of family solidarity, and the public opinion of his fellow-citizens sustained his claim. The formulas of law are connected with the creative activity of nations in the arrangement of social relations.

Even in our own day, in spite of the superiority that professional technique and legislation have acquired, it is possible sometimes to watch the formation of rules of law under the influence of business practice. Commercial law affords striking examples in this respect: it was only towards the end of the eighteenth century, under the influence especially of Lord Mansfield, that it was received in England as a recognized branch of Common Law. Before that time the usages and customs of merchants had to be established in case of dispute by the verdicts of experts — of "wise men".

The conclusion of conventions by hand-clasp and by written instruments was not invented by the lawyers, but introduced by practice. The customs of the Stock Exchange are even now at the stage of more or less fluid practices. Let us refer once more to the important law of Trade Unions: it has been established by degrees, and in face of obstinate resistance, by the pressure of workmen's groups, and these groups are still — according to English law — only privileged associations or "quasi-corporations", very powerful, but preserving the characteristic features of their non-legal origin. There is, however, no need to go back to Puchta's doctrine — a kind of "popular conviction" (*Rechtsüberzeugung*) as the mystic source of law. The true solution was indicated by Jhering, when he objected to the old historical school which sought in the past for the guiding principles in the evolution of law while this evolution was directed towards the future. It is not only tradition, it is also the orientation towards an end that characterises law and gives it value. It varies according to environment, degree of civilization, national energy, the knowledge and skill of lawyers. It adapts itself more or less well to the changes in conditions and to the growth of needs. But — whether successful or imperfect — it displays in all cases a striving towards justice conceived in relation to some ideal of social value.

II. GREEK CITIES

The exclusiveness of Greek city-institutions[1] has given rise to a fundamental misconception in regard to the treatment of international relations. It is a common error to suppose that the Greek world was deficient in this respect, that there could not be any talk of international law in societies sharply divided into a number of small republics.[2] As a matter of fact it was not so, and a closer study shows that on the contrary the world of Greek cities was particularly adapted to the development of a certain kind of international, or — to speak more correctly — intermunicipal relations. The point is that not one of these cities was really self-supporting in the sense attached to the term by Aristotle. Under stress of circumstances they could exist for some time in isolation, as it were in a state of siege or blockade. But under normal conditions each of these small political units was dependent in a high degree on supplies of goods and ideas from abroad; in the existence of every one of them the intercourse with neighbours, the exchange of native products for foreign imports, was of first-rate importance. The case of Athens may serve as an illustration. Attika was deficient in the very first element of economic life — the poor soil could not provide the corn necessary to feed its population. Hence a series of protectionist measures and prohibitions of export,[3] &c. The opening of trade routes connecting Athens with granaries in the Bosporos and in Sicily played a great part in Athenian history;[4] and at the time of its flourishing expansion Athens became a centre of international intercourse without ceasing to be the home of some 21,000 privileged citizens.

The activity of intermunicipal intercourse in religious and literary life, in games and competitions of all kinds, was one of the most

---

1. This lecture is reproduced by permission of the Oxford University Press from the text published in my *Outlines of Historical Jurisprudence*, Vol. II.
2. E.g. Laurent, *Histoire du droit des gens*.
3. Lysias, xxii; Demosthenes, xxxii.
4. Beloch, *Griechische Geschichte*, I, 395 ff.

essential and remarkable features of Greek history, and it would be impossible to understand the influence of the Homeric poems, of Ionian philosophy, of the art of Pheidias and Praxiteles,[5] without the background of this common intermunicipal organization. It is characteristic that the practice of the great national games was not entirely interrupted even by feuds between the various cities,[6] and that consultations with the oracle of Delphi were carried on at the same time by the Lakedaimonians and by their enemies in Athens and in Thebes.

Commercial relations and the juridical effects of travelling and settlement in foreign parts were not less necessary and prominent consequences of the situation. For our purpose, the inter-municipal action of the ordinary institutions of Greek States is even more important than exceptional manifestations of solidarity, and the occasions for such action in the classical period of Greek history were numberless and varied.

The practices in this respect fall naturally into two groups. There were cities which, though not at war with each other, had not established definite agreements as to the treatment of disputes between their respective citizens, and there were other cities which had come to some understanding in this respect. In the first case, apart from the intervention of patrons, by means of which a member of one State enforced claims against a member of another, recourse had to be taken to procedure by self-help, and, indeed, we commonly find men led away into captivity (ἄγειν), and property taken away by distress (φέρειν), because offended persons were seeking to obtain compensation for wrongs or to assert some right. This is termed συλᾶν in the case of distress as well as in the case of reprisals. Needless to dwell on the arbitrary character of such methods, but it must be borne in mind that such raids were not by any means simple outbursts of lawless violence. As frequently happens in ancient law, distress was used as a means of obtaining justice by self-

---

5. E. MEYER, *Geschichte des Alterturns*, iii, 433 ff.
6. Cf. HERMANN-THUMSER, *Lehrbuch der griech. Antiqu.* i, p. 78 ff. SZANTO, S. V. ἐκεχειρία in *Real-Enc.* v, 2162.

help. Another feature of the procedure was that distress or reprisals are not necessarily directed against one's opponent, but might be levelled against relatives of his, or even against his countrymen at large. Such cases were considered as a justified taking of hostages, and designated by the special term ἀνδροληψία.[7]

This form of self-help, although exceedingly common, presented obvious inconveniences, and one of the principal objects of international agreement between Greek cities was to replace it by some form of regular jurisdiction. In order to put an end to the state of natural savagery in the relations of the citizens to those of neighbouring States, one city would "grant justice"(δωσιδικία) to another. A very good illustration of such a public act is to be found in the ancient treaty (fifth century B. C.) between two Lokrian cities — Chaleion and Oiantheia — preserved on a bronze tablet in the British Museum.[8] Self-help was not abolished by it, but reduced to juridical methods.

"It is forbidden to any man of Oiantheia to carry off a foreigner on the territory of Chaleion, and to any man of Chaleion to carry off a foreigner on the territory of Oiantheia, or to seize property by way of distress.

"Whosoever distrains property belonging to a foreigner shall be allowed without exposing himself to seizure to take away the goods by sea, except from the harbour below the city. If the seizure be made without right, the fine shall be four drachmae. If the person distraining keeps the thing seized for more than ten days, he shall pay the value of it once and a half. If a man of Chaleion is a resident established more than a month at Oiantheia, and *vice versa*, he shall have recourse to the justice of the city... If the affair is carried before the judges who deal with foreigners, the foreign claimant shall choose sworn persons from among the notables, but *not* his proxenos nor any fellow-citizen. For processes involving one mina or more he shall have fifteen sworn persons, for those involving

---

7. *Real-Enc.* s. v. ἀνδροληψία.
8. MICHEL, 3.

a smaller amount he shall have nine. If a citizen pleads against another citizen in virtue of the treaty, the demiurgi (magistrates) shall choose sworn assessors from among the notables, after having taken the quintuple oath. The sworn assessors shall in their turn take the same oath, and the verdict shall follow the majority."

Even in cases of treaty relations between two cities, self-help may play a part in the defence against illegal distress or violence. The way was open in such case to the intervention of a *vindex*, to use the Roman term and notion. Striking illustration of this counter-action by any member of the contracting States may be found in the manumission inscriptions of Delphi[9] and in the inscriptions commemorating the consecration of Teos to Dionysos, accompanied by guarantees of ἀσυλία on the part of neighbouring cities.[10] The formulae are: — αὐτοσαυτὸν συλέων καὶ οἱ παρατυγχάνοντες ἀζάμιοι ὄντες καὶ ἀνυπόδικοι πάσας δίκας καὶ ζαμίας. ὁ βουλόμενος, ὁ θέλων, ὁ παρατυγχάνων κύριοι ἔστωσαν ἀφελόμενοι καὶ ἀποδιδόντες τοῖς ἀδικημένοις.

In contrast with these methods of self-help stood the system by which the citizens of a foreign city obtained a standing before the Courts of a State according to certain rules: this is described as the "granting of justice," δωσιδικία or δικαιοδοσία, and the agreements regulating the procedure in such cases were called συμβολαί or σύμβολα and the procedure itself δίκη ἀπὸ συμβόλων.[11]

When justice is "granted" to a foreigner the simplest way is to apply the laws of one or the other State according to certain rules appropriate to the various modalities of the controversy. Thus a so-called "conflict of laws" takes place. The account of the struggle between Sparta and Argos in the fifth book of Thukydides (c. 79) presents a good example of the application of this method in classical Greece. The sixth clause of the treaty of 418 B. C. provided

---

9. Griech. *Dial-Inschriften*, 1721, 1749, 1857, 1936.
10. MICHEL, 51 ff. See HITZIG, *Altgriechische Staatsverträge über Rechtschilfe*, 39, 40.
11. ARIST, *Pol.* iii, 9, p. 1289 a σύμβολα περὶ τοῦ μὴ ἀδικεῖν. See HITZIG, op. cit. 31.

that "justice shall be administered to individual citizens of each State according to their ancestral customs." This can only mean that the tribunal before which the case was brought was to apply either the law of Argos or the law of Sparta, and, as the choice of the particular law to be applied was made dependent on descent, the only outstanding question is whether it was the status of the plaintiff or of the defendant that was considered decisive. The common practice in Greece was that, *ceteris paribus*, when personality was taken as the standard of selection, litigation proceeded in accordance with the status of the defendant. The personality principle was sometimes modified by taking account of the *forum domicilii* of the defendant.[12]

In the treaty between Athens and Phaselis (395-385 B.C.)[13] two different principles are mentioned side by side. The principle of the *forum contractus* is introduced for conventions made in Athens, but on other occasions the direction of the case depends on the defendant's domicile. Conventions made outside Athens were not to be interpreted in accordance with Athenian law, and this can hardly mean anything else but the concession to the Phaselites of the application of their laws in the case of contracts made with their city.

An important consequence of the frequency and multiplicity of intermunicipal relations was the tendency of the various city customs and laws towards generalization and unification. Rules of common law grew up on an intermunicipal basis, and towards the end of the fourth century one may speak of a private inter national law of Greece, which, though not codified, was governed in most important respects by similar if not identical principles. This is stated in as many words in Demosthenes' oration against Lakritos concerning commercial laws.[14]

In the speech against Zenothemis a similarity of trade customs is implied by the fact that in a trial conducted at Athens one of the

---

12. GILBERT, Staats-Alterth., I, p. 487. Lipsius, p. 966.
13. MICHEL, 6. Cf. COLEMAN PHILLIPSON, i. 200.
14. xxxv, § 45.

parties proposes to obtain evidence as to a transaction concluded at Syrakuse, while a Massaliote trader pleads on the strength of a document executed at sea with a skipper, and the magistrates of Kephallenia order a Massaliote ship to sail to Athens in view of its original destination to that port. Nor is that community of legal principles restricted to commercial affairs, as may be gathered from Isokrates' Aiginetic speech, dealing with the validity of a will.[15]

The processes which led to the building up of a Common Law of Greece can be clearly discerned. To begin with, there was colonization, in which all the Greek cities of any importance took part. It resulted in the transfer of rules and usages across the seas to different places. Thurioi, Kerkyra, Olbia, the Chalkidike, etc., were as many centres for the spread of the customs of Athens, of Korinth, of Miletos, of Chalkis, &c.[16] The compulsory tie of political allegiance was sometimes altogether discarded, but, as in the case of the United States as regards England, the legal traditions of the metropolis persisted in the new surroundings, although with some variations in detail.

A second powerful influence brought to bear on the unification of intermunicipal law was the action of leagues and confederacies. The most potent influence in this respect was, of course, exercised by the first Athenian-Delian league.[17] Its power made itself felt through the greater part of the fifth century, and the gradual assumption by Athens of jurisdiction in important cases led necessarily to the introduction of Athenian methods and principles in the administration of law.[18] This "reception" of Attic law by the allies of Athens was, however, the effect of governmental pressure rather than that of intermunicipal agreements, and, although its

---

15. ISOKR. xix. § §12-15. Cf. E. WEISS, *Z.SS. Rom. Abth.* xxxiii. pp. 215 f.
16. For example, the treaty between the Epiknemidian Lokri and the Lokrian colonists in Naupaktos (fifth century B.C.), ROEHL, *I. G. A.* 321, MICHEL, 285. *Griech. Dial.-Inschr.* 1478.
17. MORRIS, *American Journ. Phil.*, v (5884), 298 ff.
18. H. WEBER, *Attisches Prozessrecht in den attischen Seebundsslaaten*. On the

results were permanent and important, their discussion does not lie within the scope of our inquiry. The methods adopted by the second Athenian league in the fourth century are more interesting from our point of view.[19] This alliance was framed with the distinct object of avoiding the subjugation of the allies by Athens, and, in the treaties with various members of the league, the leading city had to renounce expressly the right to keep garrisons and to acquire land within the territory of the allied commonwealths.[20] As regards jurisdiction, it was to follow the ordinary lines of the conflict of laws, while appeals had to be decided not by the Heliaea but by the Council of the League.[21]

The report of a case has been preserved in which the decision fell against an Athenian who had infringed the rule forbidding the acquisition of landed property in an allied State (*C.I.A.* II. 17). As a matter of fact, the leading city did encroach in many ways on the autonomy of the fellow-republics, and turned its hegemony to advantage in order to increase its political power. But this is matter of political history rather than of law.

The oligarchical confederation of Boiotia in the fifth century, whose organization has been made known to us in detail through the discovery of the Oxyrhynchus fragment of Theopompos' *Hellenika*,[22] was constructed on a principle of genuine representation of the eleven sections (μέρη) of the land, and the hegemony of Thebes was based mainly on the greater number of its representatives in the regional and in the central councils. Disputes between the members of the confederacy were brought before a Federal Court composed on the usual proportional basis; it is known to what

---

συμμαχία turned into an ἀρχή see Hermokrates' speech in Syrakuse. THUK, VI, 76.
19. See BUSOLT, *Der zweite attische Bund.*
20. *C. I. A.*, ii, 37, 49, 49b.
21. Cf. *C. I. A.*, iv, 2, n. 54b (Ditt. Syll.3 I, 173), ll. 45f. IV, 2, n. 88d, ll. 13f. *C. I. A.*, ii, n. 546, l. 21.
22. *Hellenica Oxyrhynchia*, ed. Grenfell and Hunt, ch. 4.

extent this Court acted as a tribunal of appeal, or of first instance, but it may be supposed that the ordinary rules as to domicile and *lex contractus* applied, subject to occasional revision of judgements by the central Court.

Apart from articles of Confederation international intercourse was conducted under customary rules and under treaties. A number of the latter have come down to us in their documentary form, and we can judge from them to what extent the device of arbitration was resorted to in this world of independent States. It was the natural outcome of conflicts between cities anxious to settle disputes by legal process.[23] The Kerkyraians complained in Athens in the course of the negotiations which preceded the Peloponnesian war that the Spartans did not want to try conclusions on equal terms according to convention, but preferred force to justice.[24] The ordinary expedient was to agree upon an umpire—either a foreign statesman like Periander or Themistokies, or, more often, a city in whose impartiality both parties had confidence.[25] The πόλις ἔκκλητος thus selected conducted the proceedings with all formalities necessary to secure careful examinations of claims and evidence. A classical example of such an arbitration is presented by the inscription commemorating the proceedings in a trial before a court of Knidos between the cities of Kos and Kalymna.[26] This case falls into the second century B. C., but there are many notices of similar proceedings on earlier occasions, and there can be no doubt that similar methods of procedure were commonly recognized and developed in the most minute particulars.[27]

---

23. M. TOD, *International Arbitration*, Oxford, 3053.
24. THUK, i, 34.
25. AISCHINES, III. DEM. xviii, 134.
26. I.F.G., I, 158 ff. Cf. TOD, op. cit., p. 49: "The inscription consists of four parts. A. The oath taken by members of the Knidian tribunal. B. Directions regarding the production of evidence and the conduct of the trial. C. A statement of the case for the claimants and of the amount of their claim. D. A record of the verdict and a list of the advocates on each side".
27. Cf. LÉCRIVAIN, s. v. ephesis in DAR. et S. TOD, op. cit., passim.

An important variety of intermunicipal justice arose when law had to be administered not by arbitral, but by municipal Courts. Such cases were of daily occurrence in connexion with commercial transactions. If a ship belonging to a Milesian citizen came to Athens and discharged a cargo owned by merchants of Smyrna, all sorts of disputes might arise out of transactions and delicts of the shippers, the crew, the passengers, the consignees. Apart from ordinary rules of conflict of laws, Athenian Courts had to take cognisance of disputes under intermunicipal agreements — δίκαι ἀπὸ συμβόλων — of customs of trade and navigation, of general principles of law and equity in the punishment of delicts and the award of compensation.[28] Unless the dispute grew into an international quarrel, it was regularly con sidered and decided by Athenian Courts — by the ναυτοδίκαι or, later on, by a section of the jury, under the chairmanship of θεσμοθέται. The procedure in these cases when they did not assume the character of public law trials (γραφαί) was of a simplified kind, as befits commercial jurisdiction. In Athens it was provided in the fourth century that the case should be tried within a month after the action had been brought.

The provision of treaties and agreements between independent States raises the fundamental question of sanctions for the fulfilment of the obligations laid down in them. Sometimes the payment of fines in case of infringement is mentioned in the text, as e. g. in the case of the treaty between Elis and Heraia[29] (588-572 B.C.) in which we find stipulated the payment of one talent of silver to the Olympian Zeus. Wagers are made in litigation with corresponding deposits to satisfy the winning party; sometimes, again, hostages are given to ensure the carrying out of the provisions; this latter expedient was, of

---

28. THUK., i, 77. Cf. LIPSIUS, *Attisches Recht und Rechtsverfahren*, p. 972.
29. *C. I. G.*, i, ii. MICHEL, I, I αἰ δὲ μὰ συνέαν τάλαντόν κ' ἀργύρο ἀποτίνοιαν τῶι Δὶ 'Ολυνπίοι.

course, chiefly used in cases of public obligations. But the principal guarantee of the fulfilment of treaties and conventions was the *oath* of the parties. Now this may mean very little or a great deal. We know by experience that interests and passions may turn the most solemn asseveration into a scrap of paper, and the history of ancient Greece provides many examples of treachery of that kind. But it would be a gross error to suppose that the religious sanction implied by the oaths and imprecations had no real meaning or weight. Its breach entailed not only loss of credit — a most important source of influence in the world — but it clashed with beliefs and moral feelings which were strongly established and powerful in the classical world. It is not for nothing that treaties, when concluded and ratified, had to be confirmed by the oath of the whole population of a State, or at least of large and influential sections of its population.

The formulae of these oaths are characteristic: they are personal and not representative, because the ancient city was a concrete reality, and not a corporation in the modern sense with the attributes of a *persona ficta*.[30] In the earlier stages of Greek history the fear of the ἄγος incurred by the violation of an oath was certainly a strong deterrent, though, of course, like all deterrents, it did not prevent occasional breaches of faith under temptation. Even in later times the religious sanction had not lost its meaning, because religion afforded the natural channel for those supermunicipal and supernational feelings which form, as it were, the second root of international law.

The claims of civilization and of humanity were not vain words for the Greeks; in spite of the narrowness of their civic organizations, they had a vivid sense of personal dignity and of moral restraint, as well as a sense of beauty and a thirst for truth. No one who has read the story of the interview between Priamos and Achilles in the *Iliad* can fail to recognize that, amidst all the horrors of ruthless fights, Greek youths were brought up to harbour humane feelings towards the unfortunate and the vanquished. The way in which Thukydides

---

30. HIRZEL, *Der Eid*.

relates the atrocities committed by his countrymen as well as by their enemies — the slaughter of Mytilene, the slaughter of Melos, the slaughter of sailors on neutral ships, is in itself a piece of evidence and a lesson. And the popular roots of these feelings were intertwined with religious conceptions. It is to the Ζεὺς ξένιος that a wanderer in a foreign land appealed for protection. It is at the sacred hearth that a refugee sought an asylum from vengeance and pursuit,[31] and when the refugee took on his lap the child of the householder, he made the latter think of what fortune might have in store for his offspring. A curious set of commandments bearing on humane conduct has come down to us in connexion with the traditional lore of a noble family in Athens, the Buzygae.[32] A similar though much shorter set of commandments was adopted by the Amphiktyonic League of Delphi and Thermopylae.[33] This League might be regarded rightly as an embryonic League of Nations; its constitution goes back to a very early period in the colonization of Greece by Hellenes — its membership[34] was restricted and its methods rudimentary, but it was an attempt to embody the notion of international justice in an organized institution. The religious authority of Delphi gave it powerful support, and it was not devoid of compulsory sanctions. In this respect its endeavours stranded, as usual, on the divergence of interests and the inequality of forces of its component members. Twice the League, in order to enforce its decrees, carried on prolonged wars with the help of coalitions of cities. In both cases these wars were made to serve the interests of the great powers — Sparta and Makedon. This is, however, a difficulty common to all states of society dominated by territorial sovereignty, a difficulty which could only be removed by the building up of a World State — a contingency very distant even in our own time.

---

31. E.g. Themistokles at Admetos' hearth. THUK, I, 136.
32. TOEPFFER, *Attische Genealogie*, p. 139.
33. Cf. as to free trade between allies, PLUT. *Perikles*, 29.
34. See BUERGEL, *Die pylaeisck-delphische Amphiktyonie*. Cf. HERMANN-THUMSER, i, 90ff.

As for the Greeks, their intermunicipal humanity was undoubtedly restricted during the early and the classical period to the circle of Hellenic civilization. The barbarians were regarded as inferior by nature; notice, for instance, Aristotle's account of the barbaric roots of slavery. But this pride of race begins to undergo a remarkable transformation towards the end of the classical age. Instead of the racial, it is the cultural aspect that is thrust into the foreground, and hereby a transition is provided to a different world, in which Hellenism appears not as a national peculiarity, but as a badge of civilization. One of the forerunners of the Hellenistic age, Isokrates, has expressed this in as many words:[35] "Our city has so far surpassed the rest of mankind in power of thought and speech that her disciples have become the teachers of the rest; she has made the name of Hellene seem to belong no longer to the race, but to the mind, so that the name is given to those who share in our culture more than to those who share the common blood."

---

35. Isokr. iv, 50.

III. THE *JUS GENTIUM* OF THE ROMANS

A mighty causeway leading into a dim past is supplied by Roman Law. Students are still made to read Justinian's *Primer*; the Scots, the Dutch, the people in Ceylon, have still to reckon with the opinions of Paul and of Ulpian in their Courts; even where English or French or German law is supreme, the mode of juridical thinking is to a large extent permeated with ideas and habits derived from the Romans by innumerable links with the past. Surely this astonishing fact is more than an accident, more than an acknowledgment of technical skill: it must be connected with some social features of this system which have made it the vehicle of powerful tendencies of the human mind. This view is more than a mere guess: it is clearly revealed in the manifestation of Roman Law as an agent of universal culture which resulted in the growth of a common law of the Roman Empire, the *jus gentium*.

In this case I should like to start from the specific features of the legal development and to treat of the social type to which it corresponds at the close of my lecture.

I need not dwell on the earlier stage of Roman legal history — on the growth of the *jus civile*, the law of Roman citizens, as it is embodied for instance in the famous XII Tables; it presents another example of the city type illustrated by Greek jurisprudence in my former lecture, dominated by the idea of the City— an exclusive political club of citizens. The only side of this legal formation which must be noticed is the exceptional logical precision of the machinery provided by the jurisdiction of Roman magistrates. It is in the treatment of the relations between citizens belonging to different commonwealths that Roman law achieved far-reaching and permanent results. In the beginning the cities of Italy had worked out their legal arrangements on the narrow lines of municipal life, and the means they were able to devise for protecting business relations with other cities were derived from private protection by influential citizens (*hospites*) and from religious sources, (*Fas*, τὰ ὅσια) or from treaties establishing reciprocity. With the neighbouring Latin cities the Romans were able to deal to a great extent on the basis of common juridical institutions like the *mancipatio* and the *legis actio*.¹ When the circle of these international relations widened they worked out certain rules for the application of different systems of law. The two treaties between Rome and Carthage concluded in the third century B.C. may serve as examples of such arrangements.

The juridical questions arising out of such relations were of the nature of what is termed *conflicts of law*. If a Roman and a Carthaginian had concluded a bargain, was that bargain to be interpreted and carried out in conformity with Roman or with Carthaginian law? The laws to be applied were in any case those of one or the other of the cities, not a law common and superior to both.

By the side of this procedure aiming at a choice between conflicting laws grew another method for settling disputes — procedure by *recuperatio*.² It was employed in cases where there was no treaty, no *foedus* to start with, or where the parties to the treaty had agreed to refer disputes to a court of compulsory arbitration. The process of "recovery" takes place when there exists a legal agreement between foreign states that private property is to be rendered to individuals and recovered by them.

If matters had continued in this state the controversies between citizens and foreigners, though characteristic for the course of municipal jurisdiction more or less on the same line with the methods employed usually in the Greek cities, would have remained without much significance from the point of view of general civilization. But the aspect of things changed entirely when Rome conquered the Eastern and Southern shores of the Mediterranean. It became the centre of the world's commerce and culture; it was driven to expand the narrow framework of its civil law and of its municipal jurisdiction. This process began in the Vth century of the City (third century B.C.) its first conspicuous manifestation being the institution

---

1. GAIUS i, 119; ii, 24; v, 16.
2. FESTUS, de verborum significat. (TEUBNER p. 343. Reciperatio est, cum inter civitates lex convenit, ut res privatae reddantur singulis recuperenturque.

of the *praetor peregrinus* in 247 B.C. By the middle of the third century, A. D. it was virtually completed.

In principle, Roman courts, even when admitting claims and defences of foreigners on a footing of equality — e. g. under a *foedus* granting *commercium* — could not grant them the characteristic remedies of the law of the Quirites except by resorting to fiction. If the foreigner complained, for instance of damage that had been done by some miscreants on the road to cattle which he had brought to market, the Praetor could allow him the action *ex lege Aquilia* (*de damno injuria data*) by instructing the judge of fact to examine the case and to condemn or to absolve without paying attention to the personal status of the plaintiff: the latter was regarded, by way of fiction, as if he had been a citizen. In the same way he could obtain the benefit of fictitious status in defending the possession of a piece of land which he had occupied and cultivated. In this last case two fictions would intervene — that of citizenship and that of perfecting the acquisition by long usage (*usucapio*).

Such devices were used on certain few occasions. More usual was the recourse to *equitable* principles, which could be best established by keeping to the broad lines of juridical ideas more or less common to all. This was easiest as regards obligations — good faith and consent became fundamental requirements of such transactions between citizens and foreigners. The Empire did not attempt to level all local peculiarities as regards law. Even Caracalla's constitution of 212 did not create a unified system. It did not affect the *dediticii* and even the Roman citizens of various provinces continued to follow popular customs of their own. The lawyers who administered the law were not less Roman in that period than they were before, but they started on a new track, quite distinct from, though sometimes parallel to, that of the city law (*jus civile*); they recognized a common law of nations (*jus gentium*). The writers on Roman jurisprudence tell us of a number of most important contracts and actions in defence of them, which were derived from the *jus gentium*. Roman Law became international as a combination of various currents of national laws. It may be noticed that this private international law was a *jus gentium* and not a *jus civitatum*. That means that it was built up by means of generalization from principles recognized by various nations — the Greeks, the Egyptians, etc. not by reference to specific legislation say of Athens, of Miletos, of Syracuse. The essential contrast between the strict forms required by the *jus civile* and the liberal interpretation of rules and conventions on the ground of international usages may be illustrated, for instance, by Gaius' remarks in his *Institutes* on the various kinds of promises.³

"The contract by means of the words of a binding promise *Dari Spondes? Spondeo* is peculiar to Roman citizens. Other forms of promise are part of the law of nations and so hold good among all men whether Roman citizens or foreigners; and even if they are translated into Greek,... they still hold good among Roman citizens provided that the latter (the R. citizens) understand the Greek language; and conversely if they are uttered in Latin still they hold good among foreigners if these foreigners understand the Latin language. But this contract by the formula *Dari Spondes? Spondeo* is so exclusively peculiar to Roman citizens that it cannot even be translated properly into Greek, although the Forms are said to be derived from the Greek".

The object of such innovations in contrast with Ancient Roman rules was expressly to treat relations from the point of view of reasonableness and equity which would be especially applicable to all varieties of the human race. Natural reasonableness is the starting

---

3. GAIUS, Inst. iii, 93. Sed haec quidem verborum obligatio Dan Spondes? Spondeo propria civium Romanorum est; ceterae vero iurus gentium sunt, itaque inter omnes homines, sive cives Romanos sive peregrinos, valent; et quamvis ad Graecam vocem expressae fuerint... etiam hae tamen inter cilves Romanos valent, si modo Graeci sermonis intellectum habeant; et a contrario quamvis Latine enuntientur, tamen etiam inter peregrinos valent, si modo Latini sermonis intellectum habeant, at illa verborum obligatio Dari Spondes? Spondeo adeo propria civium Romanonum est, ut ne quidem in Graecum sermonem per intenpretationem pnoprie transfenni possit, quamvis dicatur a Graeca voce figurata esse.
Cf. MITTEIS, *Rom. Privatr.* i, 62 ff.
CUQ. *Institutions juridiques*, 14.

point of the *jus gentium*. Take as an instance *tradition*, as a method of transferring property. See D. xli, D. 645, I. 9, 3.

In the same spirit and under the same generic reference to *jus gentium* are treated *sale* (D. xviii, I, 2, xix, 2, I) *lease and hire* (D. xix, 2, I) *partnership* (Gaius *Inst.* iii, 154) etc.[4]

"In all those cases in which the formula "in good faith" is added or "as ought to be done in honest dealing between honest men" and especially in judgments about a wife's property in which occurs the formula "as is best and fairest for her" the jurisconsults ought to be ready to intervene. It is they who have laid down the definitions of fraud, good faith, equity, the duties of partner to partner, the mutual obligations of one who has conducted another person's affairs and of that person himself, of agent and principal, of husband to wife and of wife to husband."

Tryphoninus presents in strong relief the notions of good faith and honesty as the decisive principles in the application of the law of nations.[5]

"The good faith which is demanded in the case of contracts looks for the highest equity; but do we estimate that according to the law of nations only or in connection with civil and praetorian rules?

---

4. CICERO, *Top.* 17, 65-6. In omnibus igitur eis judiciis, In quibus ex fide bona est additum, ubi etiam *ut inter bonos bene agier oportet* in pnimisque in arbitrio rei uxoriae, in quo est *qvod eivs aeqvivs* parati ei esse debent. Illi dolum malum, illi fidem bonam, illi aequum bonuml, illi quid socium socio, quid eum qui negotia aliena curasset ei cuius ea negotia fuissent, quid eum qui man dasset, eumve cui mandatam esset, alterum alteri praestare oporteret, quid virum uxori quid uxorem viro tradiderunt. Cf. E. WEISS, s. v. *jus gentium Real Enc. of Pauly-Wissowa*, x, 128.

5. *Dig.* XVI, 3, 31. Bona fides quae in contractibus exigitur aequitatem summam desiderat: sed eam utrum aestimamus ad merum ius gentium an vero cern praeceptis civilibus et praetoriis? veluti reus capitalis iudicii deposuit apud te centum: is deportatus est, hona eius publicata sunt: utrumne ipsi haec reddenda an in publicum deferenda sint? si tantum naturale et gentium ius intuemur, ei qui dedit restituenda sunt; si civile ius et legum ordinem magis in publicum deferenda sunt.

Suppose that the accused on a capital charge has deposited with you a hundred sesterces. He is banished and his property is confiscated by the State. Ought the money to be repaid to him or should it be handed over to the State? If we consider natural law of nations, it should be restored to the man who gave it to you. If we regard civil law and legal procedure it should be handed over to the State."

These legal relations and actions mostly belong to one definite group: they arise from business transactions and contractual obligations, and are especially applicable in the life of a business community: they are more particularly fitted for the regulation of commercial intercourse and assign particular importance to the moral basis of social intercourse and credit namely *good faith*. Another topic on which the *jus gentium* is brought to bear is the legal situation of husband and wife arising from mixed marriages between Romans and foreign women or *vice versa* between foreigners and Roman women. These marriages were *matrimonia non justa*, unions not safeguarded by civil law: they were, however, not a variety of concubinage: with the spread of Roman power and the influx of foreigners into Italy they became more and more frequent, and the Praetor formed a special action — *de re uxoria* — to protect the property of the wife under *jus gentium*. Besides these main instances the *jus gentium* was appealed to in miscellaneous cases to support claims derived from general considerations of justice supposed to be common to various nations. A notable instance is registered by Quintilian as regards dispute concerning succession.[6]

He discusses the treatment of a well known "controversy" of the schools in which two sons are claiming the estate of their father who has died intestate. There are particular legal complications, the

---

6. QUINT. *Inst. Or.* vii, i, 42-63.
46. At qui naturam sequetur, illa cogitabit profecto. primo hoc dicturuni rusticum: "Pater intestatus duos nos filios reliquit, partem iure gentium peto". Quis tam imperitus, quis tam procul a litteris, quin sic incipiat, etiamsi nescierit, quid sit propositio? Hanc communem omnium legem leviter adornabit ut iustam.

point of interest here being that one of the claimants bases his claim on the *jus gentium* and this is recognised as a natural procedure for him to adopt. "My father, he will say, "dying intestate has left two sons, my brother and me, I claim my share by the law of nations." The pleader, says Quintilian, will dwell on and amplify the justice of this law of nations.

The introduction of this new body of laws — the *jus gentium* — was not brought about by legislative acts: the *leges* and *senatus consulta* applied directly to civil law and touched the intercourse between nations only in an indirect and subsidiary way. The edicts of the praetors and of the governors who wielded the administrative *imperium* in the province referred frequently to rules based on natural reasonableness and assisted materially in establishing them. But these edicts themselves were in no way the product of the magistrates' personal opinion: normally, they presented the juridical results of ideas elaborated by business practice and by professional analysis. And it is in the domain of the *jus gentium* that these sources of law conceived as authoritative opinions of jurists (*responsa prudentium*) found their widest application. Cicero (*Top.* 17, 65-6) traces expressly the development of the doctrines of good faith to the action of jurisconsults (see quotation on pp. 91-92).

I need hardly explain the value of the *responsa* in this connection. Although not obligatory for the court at which they were invoked, they guided the magistrates in the same way as judicial precedents guide the Bench in a trial under English Common Law. The praetor or proconsul who would have decided a case as to the validity of a sale or the responsibility of principles or agents in opposition to the opinion of a Labeo would have been a bold man and even if learned lawyers differed the magistrate had at any rate some authority to rely upon. The process was not different in substance at the time of the Emperors, although in some cases rulers of great judicial experience, like Antoninus Pius or Marcus Aurelius laid down juridical views of their own, when sitting in Court. On the whole, edicts of the praetors, of the *Ædiles curules* (as to market disputes), of the governors of provinces were closely connected with advice from jurists and with business practice. The influence of the latter forms an interesting subject by itself — a subject which finds a striking parallel in the development of English Law. The so-called Law Merchant grew up distinctly out of the observation of business usages which, apart from coercion and sanction, expressed the views and habits of traders and customers. Before it was declared to be necessary at law for the validity of a contract of sale to make and to accept a preliminary payment in the shape of a "sale shilling" this token of the concluded sale was used by parties as a customary precaution. Before the subtle rules as to the moment when a contract was deemed to be concluded were evolved by law there made its appearance the usage that contracting parties, for example a bride and a bridegroom, symbolised the consent of their wills by joining hands. In this way the background to the rights and claims under *jus gentium* is formed by innumerable business transactions of a non-litigious nature, subsequently revised, defined and analysed in the brunt of controversy before the Courts.

Let us consider more closely one or two of the specific institutions of the *jus gentium*. The treatment of sale is characteristic enough. According to the *jus civile* to buy or to sell an object of some value — an ox, a slave, a house — was a solemn and cumbersome affair. The property had to be handed over by hand to the purchaser in the presence of citizens as witnesses and of a sixth, who had to hold the scales on which the ingots of bronze constituting or symbolizing the price of the purchased object were to be weighed. Even when other kinds of goods were sold which did not require handing over as objects of bargains, sales affecting ownership according to the Laws of the Quirites were necessarily bound up with immediate tradition, the reception of an equivalent in money and the obligation of the vendor to warrant, to stand *security* for the transaction incase of eviction. Even apart from the archaic symbols of *aes et libra* pointing to an age when there was no coined money in circulation and its place was taken by weighed pieces of metal, the stiffness, the formalism and the complicated responsibility attached to the transaction, were suitable only to the restricted traffic of a peasant commonwealth. For the development of commerce on a large scale other means were required—above all greater flexibility and freedom. And these requirements were satisfied by the substitution of a consensual agreement as to sale under the rules of *emptio venditio*, a contract built up mainly by recognition of international usage: as bargains with Greeks, with Egyptians, with Syrians became more and more frequent, the praetors and the provincial governors had to conform to the habits of the hellenistic community opposed to formalism. There was no necessity for a sacrament or of witnesses and a symbolic dramatic performance connected with the sale, there was no necessity for immediate payment, the way was open to credit operations and conditions as to terms of payment, there were no absolute requirements of warranty, and the requirements of good faith and right value were to be satisfied in other ways — by checking fraud (dolus). It is impossible, of course, to determine to what extent the development of credit and of transactions based on good faith is to be attributed to the natural progress of intercourse among the Romans themselves, and how far it was influenced by business relations with Greeks and Orientals, who had long practised methods of this kind. Both have to be taken into account.[7]

I have chosen sale for an example of the process of transfor mation, but analogous alterations take place all along the line in the law of obligations arising out of contracts. Everywhere ancient municipal formalism gives way before the spiritual standard of consent, of free will, prevailing among the trading com monwealths of the East — both Greek and Phoenician. Another consequence of this transformation may be recognized in our own practice. In our law there is a special department of so- called conveyancing — it deals with the proper and provident way of drawing up instruments conveying rights to be transferred from one person to another. Notaries draw up these conveyances in Continental countries, solicitors prepare them in the domain of English law. In this case written instruments are the normal vehicles for transactions of any

---

7. Cf. MUCIUS SCAEVOLA (Caecilius) ap. GELLIUM, xx, i, 41. Hanc fidem majores nostri ... in negociorum contractibus sanxerunt maximeque in pecuniae mutua clone atque commercio.

considerable importance, especially transactions as to land. Now, this vital importance of writing in the legislation of transactions is anything but a primaeval institution. The normal way of declaring will and ascertaining its exact form and conditions was in Ancient Rome the ceremonial act, the solemn drama culminating in a declaration (*nuncupatio*), an avowal (*in jure cessio*), in legal selfhelp (*pignoris capio, manus injectio*) in a compromise or agreement (pactum), in a promise (*stipulatio*). Acts in law were indeed acted by the subject of rights concerned in them. This was already quite different in the hellenised East when the Romans came into close contact with it. Declarations, dispositions, agreements were executed in writing, the will was expressed by an inscription on a stone, on wood, on a piece of leather, on a dyptych of tablets covered with wax, joined on their inner sides and secured with seals or subscriptions of witness on the outside. Last, but not least, legal instruments were drawn up on sheets of papyrus. In this case again, the everyday conditions of business suggested the appropriate form for legal acts in law. The written contract, the written testament came to take the place of the acted agreement, of the testament witnessed by the general assembly of the people (*comitia*) or by the Army in its war attire (*in procinctu*). And neither the Roman magistrates nor the Masters of legal doctrines, the Jurisprudentes were so pedantic as not to recognize the advantages of these methods of expressing and establishing will and consent. Instruments which were originally meant to be memoranda as to actual events became gradually the means of embodying acts in Law.

It is impossible to trace exactly how much is to be ascribed to the direct influence of Greek and Oriental legal usage, and how far, on the other hand, these may have been influenced by practices derived from public law and worked out specifically under administrative officers like the censors or the aediles. Even more difficult would it be to assign a definite measure to direct loans of foreign customs and to the indirect stimulating effects on the mind of Roman magistrates of meeting new and peculiar methods in the countries of ancient civilisation which had been conquered by Rome. However this may be, it is certain that thanks to Hellenism as arranged by Rome, the permanent way was created as it were, and the rails laid for business intercourse on the lines of free trade which has stood, in a sense, the wear and tear of some 20 centuries. What happened in that eventful age of the Roman Empire in the sphere of material interests and material intercourse was to a great extent akin to what took place in the domain of the mind, where Rome paved the ways for the spread of Eastern beliefs and Greek speculation in matters of religion.

We may differ in estimating the influence of environment and of personal factors in these processes, but there can be no doubt as to the universal character of the results achieved. It is not only by the more or less elemental working of circumstances or by an unconscious collecting of particular rules that this stand point was reached. It is not difficult to discern the leading idea which pervaded the whole process in all its details; Roman lawyers have tried repeatedly to give expression to this dominant idea:[8]

"All nations governed by laws and customs use partly their own law, partly that which is common to all men. The law which each people lays down for itself is peculiar to it and is called civil law as belonging to the city, but that which natural reason has established among all men is observed equally among all peoples and is called the law of nations as being that law which is used by all nations. And so the Roman people uses partly its own and partly the law common to all men."[9]

This passage and similar ones follow closely the statement in Aristotle's *Rhetoric* and in the *Nikomachean Ethics* on the contrast

---

8. Cf. BAVIERA, *Archivio Giuridico*, lxi.
9. GAIUS, *Inst.* i, I. Omnes populi, qui legibus et moribus reguntur, partini suo proprio, partim communi omnium hominuni jure utuntur: nam quoci quisque populus ipse sibi jus constituit, id ipsius proprium est vocaturque jus civile, quasi jus pro. prium civitatis; quod vero neturalis ratio inter omnes homines constituit, id apud omnes populos peraeque custoditur vocaturque ius gentium, quasi quo lure omnes gentes utuntur; et populus itaque Romanus partim suo proprio, partim communi omnium hominum iure utitur.

between natural law which is common to all (*κοινός*) and particular laws (*ἴδιοι νόμοι*). It is evident that educated Romans jurists were well acquainted with the speculations of Greek philosophers as to a common law of nature. But this fact does not in any way justify the view that the *jus gentium* was merely a theoretical conception used in jurisprudence for the sake of a classification of various kinds of law; although his point of view has been taken up in literature by eminent authorities.[10] At the back of the term stood a large and important class of legal principles applicable to the regulation of business intercourse between the nationalities of the Empire. The notion that these principles formed a common law based on usually accepted equitable estimates and customs is particularly interesting on account of its correspondence to the common law of the English speaking peoples, which was formulated by judicial authority in dealing with cases supplied by a society composed of groups with varying degrees of political standing and cultural development.[11]

The Roman lawyers were not altogether successful in their attempt at theoretical generalization: their definitions of the *jus gentium* run sometimes perilously near other departments of jurisprudence, especially equity and the so-called law of nature.[12] But some confusion in details does not destroy the fundamental conception. The keystone is to be found in the community of intercourse between the free. The *jus civile* is necessarily a law for Roman citizens (Quirites); the *jus naturale* embraces the whole of mankind and, in some respects, even animals (Ulpian). The *jus gentium* comprises within its compass the free men (*liberi*) and excludes slaves. For this reason even persons deprived of civic rights and standing in a commonwealth, but possessed of personal freedom, are protected by the *jus gentium*: a quotation from the Digest may illustrate the distinction.[13]

---

10. E. G. BARON, *Peregrinenrecht und Jus gentium*, LENEL, in Holtzendorf Kohler's *Rechtsencyclopaedie*.
11. MITTEIS, *Romisches Privatrecht*, E. WEISS, in *Pauly Wissowa's Real-encyclopaedie s. v. jus gentium*.
12. Cf. H. NETTLESHIP, *Contributions to Latin Lexicography*, p. 500 ff.
13. MARCIANUS *Dig.* xlviii. 1917.

"Also certain persons are ἀπόλιδες, that is without a state: such as those who are condemned in perpetuity to public service and those who are transported to an island, so that while they have not those rights which belong to civil law, they still have those which belong to the law of nations."[13]

Thus the *jus gentium* appears as the common law of intercourse between free individuals and this explains its lasting influence in jurisprudence. It forms the main stock of private international law in societies constructed on the principle of free individual association. This seems the clue to its reception in modern States. It proved a powerful auxiliary in the struggle of modern nations against class privileges, provincial separatism and arbitrary prerogative.

In conclusion I should like to refer to a passage which sums up the principal features of the *jus gentium*.[14]

"But civil law derives its name from each individual state, as for instance that of the Athenians; if one wished to call the laws of Solon or Dracon the civil law of the Athenians he would not be wrong. Thus too we call the law used by the Roman people the civil law of the Romans, or that used by the Qui rites the civil law of the Quirites; for the Romans are called Quirites after Quirinus. But when we do not add the name specifying the state we mean our own law... The law of nations on the other hand is common to all the human race. For under pressure of usage and human needs the human races have set up certain rules for themselves; wars too have arisen, and captivities have followed, and enslavements, which are contrary to the law of nature (for by the law of nature all men were from the beginning born free); and as the result of this law of nations almost all contracts (agreements) have been introduced, purchase and sale, lease and hire, partnership, deposit, loan, and count less others."

---

14. MARCIANUS. *Inst.* i. 2. 2. Sed ius quidem civile ex unaquaque civitate appellatur, veluti Atheniensium; nam si quis velit Solonis vel Draconis leges appellare ius civile Atheniensium, non erraverit. Sic enim et ius, quo populus Romanus utitur, ius civile Romanorum appellamus vel ius Quiritium, quo Quirites utuntur; Romani enim Quirites a Quirino appellantur. Sed quoties

non addimus nomen, cuius sit civitas, nostrum jus significamus... Ius autem gentium omni humano generi commune est. Nam usu exigente et humanis necessitatibus gentes humanae quadam sibi constituerunt; bella etenim orta sunt, et captivitates secutae, et servitutes, quae sunt naturali iuri contraniae (iure enim naturali omnes homines ab initio liberi nascebantur); et ex hoc iure gentium omnes paene contractus introducti sunt, ut emptio venditio, locatio conductio, societas, depositum, mutuum et alii innumerabiles.

IV. THE WORLD STATE OF MEDIAEVAL CHRISTENDOM

When the fabric of the antique civilisation broke down under the onslaught of the barbarians, a slow process of reconstruction began by which natural economics and legal order were built up again in scattered local self-protecting units, although the imperial intercourse of previous times did not disappear without leaving some traces of its existence. As in the very beginning of human evolution, social consciousness was dominated by religious ideas: every thing in life was connected in some way with supernatural beliefs and aspirations; every manifestation of human activity was measured by the standard of divine commandments. In contrast with the disruption of the material world into a multitude of political fragments — manors, boroughs, gilds — mankind held fast to the conception of a catholic community — the Church, towering over petty interests and civil strife. It pointed out the way towards salvation in a better world — to the City of God — and for this reason it claimed the right to direct the conduct of men in the earthly city, the *Civitas terrena*. Characteristically enough the theocratic ideal of social life was not restricted to the Christian States established on the ruins of Rome; it was also the moving force in the East: the conquering wave of the Khalifate rose high under a rival standard of universal religion. The Carolingian defenders of the Christian faith and the Crusaders, met on the battlefields of Poitiers and of Antioch warriors inspired by fervent religious zeal and held together by a compact theocratic organisation. We are told that the soldiers of Mohavia charged in the battle against the host of Au with scraps of the Koran attached to their spears. If ever, this was the time for the raising of a Super-State, towering over all cleavages of nationality, class and political boundaries. If ever, this was the epoch for attempts to bridge over dissensions by means of a spiritual rule. The attempt was made in Western Europe by the Popes and it could not fail to produce momentous consequences in the domain of international relations.

It is interesting to note that the political theory of the mediaeval theocracy started definitely in the minds of its foremost representatives from the teaching of the City Commonwealth, but was carried one step further. "The Philosopher" (Aristotle) had shown that men are social beings constrained to join in families, in tribal villages and in Cities in order to attain welfare in a self-sufficient union. The schoolmen added one more link to the argument by pointing out that even cities are not self-sufficient and that human intercourse reaches self-sufficiency only in the world union of mankind.

Mankind must therfore be considered as one body politic: its life depends on the unity of its members quite as much as the existence of an individual. The living and real State is one in heaven and ought to be one on earth. St. Augustine and Gregory VII traced the history of the *civitas terrena* from Adam's fall and from Cain's fratricide, but the prevailing view of the Scholastic doctors was: nature has created the thumb for one purpose, and the hand for another purpose, and the arms for yet another, and man for a purpose different from all those. In the same way nature has contrived the single individual for one purpose, and the household for another, and the cluster of neighbours for yet another and the city for another again, and the Kingdom for another, and lastly the eternal God called forth into existence for a special purpose the generality of mankind. There is therefore a special function of universal mankind, which neither a single man, nor a household, nor a village nor a city can fulfil.[1]

As in the organic life of the individual, body and soul are equally necessary elements, but not equally important ones. The spirit is the

---

1. The deduction is tersely stated by DANTE, *De Monarchia*, i, c. 3: Et ad evidentiam elus quod quaeritur, advertendum, quod quemadmodum est finis aliquis ad quem natura producit pollicem, et alius ab hoc ad quem manum totam, et rursus alius ab utroque ad quem brachium, aliusque ab omnibus ad quem totum hominem; sic alius est finis ad quem singularem hominem, alius ad quem ordinat domesticam communitatem, alius ad quem viciniam, et alius ad quem civitatem, et alius ad quem regnum, et denique ultimus ad quem universaliter genus humanum Deus aeternus arte sua, quae natura est, in esse producit...

ruling principle and the view that the Church which embodies the spiritual elements of the community is called upon to direct human society was strictly logical. "As man cannot achieve his end, which is to enjoy God, by his own human virtue, but only through the power of God — it belongs not to man, but to God to lead him to that end. And this leadership appertains to a King who is not only a man, but a God, namely to our Lord Jesus Christ — From him is derived Royal Priesthood. In order that the spiritual may be distinct from the temporal, the Royal Office is not entrusted to the Kings of the earth, but to the Priest, and especially to the Supreme Priest, the successor of Peter, the vicar of Christ, the Bishop of Rome, to whom all the Kings of the Christian people should be subject, as to the Lord Jesus Christ himself, because those who are to take care of the subsidiary aims ought to be subject to him to whom appertains the care of the highest aim, and they should follow the Imperial leadership."[2]

This power of direction is conceived not as an absolute and all-pervading government, but as a superior guidance to which the material interests and forces have to conform and in which they have to seek a solution of their disputes and conflicts. The familiar expression of such relations between the spiritual and the secular power is given in the doctrine of the *two swords*.

In a canto of the *Purgatorio* (xvi, 106 ff.) Dante has given us the secular version of the parable. The comparison sounded quite differently in the mouth of a versifier who certainly was no match for Dante as a poet, but who expressed the feelings of the partizans

---

...Est ergo aliqua propria operatio humanae universitatis, ad quem ipsa universitas hominum in tanta multitudine ordinatur, ad quam quidem operationem nec homo unus, nec domus una, nec una vicinia, nec una civitas, nec regnum particulare pertingere potest.

Under the pen of Thomas Aquinas, the same kind of argument is used to justify the Universal rule of the Church.

2. THOMAS AQUINAS, *de regimine principum*, i, c. 15.

of papacy with considerable force.³ The conceptions which inspired the author of these doggerel rhymes matured eventually in the well known doctrine of papal supreme power in secular as well as in spiritual matters which produced as one of its most extreme manifestations Boniface VIII's famous bull "Ilnam Sanctam."⁴

The decisions in the course of the struggle were to a great extent affected by conditions of fact — by the feudal and municipal opposition to the Emperors, by the counter-poise of Norman and French politics against the aggrandisement of the Imperial power;

---

3. FIGGIS, *Respublica Christiana*. Transactions of the Royal Series III, v. 5. 1911, p. 81:

> Ergo vel ecclesiae membrum non dicetur
> Caesar, vel pontifici summo supponetur.
>
> Major et antiquior est imperialis
> Dignitas quam cleri sit vel pontificalis,
> "Major" dico tempore, semper enim malis
> Regibus subiacuit terra laycalis.
>
> Imperator Esau major quidem natu,
> Papa quidem Jacob est, minor enim statu
>
> Ille sceptro rutilat, iste potentatu,
> Ille major viribus, iste dominatu.
>
> Caesar habet gladium sed materialem,
> Hunc eundem pontifex, sed spiritualem.

4. Extr. comm. i, 8, i.

... "Unam sanctam ecciesiam catholicam et ipsam apostolicam, urgente fide credere cogimur et tenere ... quae unum corpus mysticum repraesentat, cuius caput Christus Christi vero Deus. In qua unus Dominus, una fides, unum baptisma...

... Haec est tunica ille Domini inconsutilis, quae scissa non fuit, sed sorte provenit. Igitur ecclesiae unius et unicae unum corpus, et unum caput, non duo capita, quasi monstrum, Christus videlicet et Christi vicarius Petrus, Petrique successor, dicente Domino ipsi Petro: Pasce oves meas.

... In hac eiusque potestate duos esse gladios, spiritualem videlicet et temporalem evangelicis dictis instruimur. Nam dicentibus apostolis: "ecce but at the back of these material conditions stood the immense influence of a dominating cultural idea — the belief in the spiritual leadership of Roman hierarchy. As long as the claim of the Popes to organize the Christian world was contested by the semi-barbaric Emperors, the successors of St. Peter had much the best of the game. They were stronger in theory and better fitted to put theory into practice. The tables were turned against them when their great enterprise in the conduct of foreign policy — the Crusades against Islam — had signally failed and when instead of the bastard Empire of the Hohenstaufens they were confronted by kings of consolidated National States — by Philip the Fair in France, by Edward III in England. Our present task consists, however, in tracing the way in which the Popes conceived and treated international relations in the epoch of their victories.

The principle put forward by them as the basis of the society of Christian polities was the principle of *federation*. They did not attempt to introduce an impracticable and uniform government from the centre, they admitted to the full the variety of local political organizations, but they tried to introduce harmony into the life of these various bodies: the great ideal of peace had been proclaimed emphatically both by them and by their political opponents. We may again turn to Dante for a passionate expression of this leading idea: "It is evident that man kind should strive to fulfil its almost divine work freely and easily in peace and quiet. It is clear therefore that universal peace is the greatest good that can be provided for our happiness. This is what sounded to the shepherds from heaven — not wealth, not might, not honours, not long life, not health, not strength, not beauty — but peace, the heavenly host proclaimed: Glory be to God on high, and peace to men of good will on earth."[5]

---

gladii duo hic",... Certe, qui in potestate Petri temporalem gladium esse negat, male verbum attendit Domini proferentis: "Converte gladium tuum in vaginam". Uterque ergo gladius est in potestate ecclesiae".
5. DANTE, *De Monarchia*, i, c. 4. Patet quod genus humanum in quietate sive

One of the most tangible results of the unceasing activity of the Church in the cause of peace had been the propaganda in favour of the truce of God. In spite of many disappointments and failures the movement against private wars initiated by the Church did not remain sterile and led gradually to a relative restriction of local feuds.

More ambitious and more difficult were the cases of intervention in conflicts conducted on a larger scale. In 1079 Pope Gregory VII insisted on the submission of the brothers of the Danish king to his overlordship and prohibited a division of the country which would have been detrimental to the interests of Christianity in the North. In the same year he decided as supreme judge a dispute between the sons of the Count of Barcelona and reminded them of the necessity of concord between Christian princes faced by Islam.

In the course of his controversy with Philip Augustus of France Innocent III formulated the pretensions of the papacy to intervene in conflicts between princes in the following way: Was it not the mission of the successors of St. Peter to establish peace among men? Even if the Pope had no right to intervene in feudal matters, his jurisdiction had to be recognized as to sin (ratione peccati). It remained to be seen whether Philip had not sinned by disregarding the rights of John his vassal.[6]

As to the methods employed by the Pope in these international disputes, they were derived from various sources. In his capacity as the supreme arbitrator of the Christian world the Pope claimed the right to settle the most intricate and important national and international conflicts. Although in their struggle with the Emperors

---

tranquillitate pacis ad proprium suum opus, quod fere divinum est manifestum est, quod pax universalis est optimum eorum, quae ad nostram beatitudinem ordinatur. Hinc est, quod pastoribus de sursum sonuit, non divitiae, non voluptates, non honores, non longitudo vitae, non sanitas, non robur, non pulchritudo; sed pax. Inquit enim caelestis militia: "Gloria in altissimis Deo, et in terra pax hominibus bonae voluntatis."

6. See LUCHARE, *Les royaumes vassaux*, pp. 251, 254, 259.

the Popes tried to weaken the feudal notions of fealty by exempting vassals from sworn obligations, they surround themselves with a circle of vassals.

This expedient was not well chosen from a theoretical point of view: it is in the nature of an opportunistic use of accidental advantages of position in the feudal world. A much more formidable weapon was provided by the pastoral leadership of the Pope. As the appointed teacher and guardian of faith and morals he wielded the terrible scourges of excommunication and interdict.[7]

Another side of the juridical power claimed by the Roman Curia and conceded to a great extent by public opinion and legal custom was the *extra-territorial* jurisdiction of the Canon Law in relations which affect some of the most important sides of social life — e. g. marriage, succession, testaments, trusts, charities, corporations, agreements, etc. It would be out of the question for us to treat of these various applications of Canon Law and Ecclesiastical jurisdiction at any length. But it is clear that the existence of that large body of law derived not from State legislation or local custom, but from a spiritual organization whose power was not limited by existing frontiers and territorial divisions, was in itself a factor of primary importance from an international point of view. The adjustment of the juridical ideas and institutions which had grown up on the extra-territorial soil to the Common Law of England or the practices of the French parliaments or the statutes and customs of the Italian Cities was a task of great importance, productive of incessant conflicts.

The treatment of marriage and of family relations derived from it may serve as an example. The Church considered the tie between the spouses to be a sacramental union by which two human beings were fused into one. For this reason the indissolubility of *rightful* matrimony was insisted upon and at the same time great latitude was allowed as regards *annulment* by the authority of the Pope. The widest possible application of the marriage tie in practice as against

---

7. PANDOLF in the Annals of Burton, 1212. On the Interdict in England in 1213 see *Annals of Coventry*, ii, 108.

spurious and illegitimate unions was also the object of propaganda by the Church.

In this policy it had to meet various currents of popular customs and professional doctrines which were very difficult to conquer. As against the sacrament stood the ancient treatment of marriage as a contract of betrothal negotiated primarily between the kindred of the bride on one side, the bridegroom and his kinsmen on the other. The conditions as to the conclusion, consummation and breach of such *wedding* were peculiar, and the chief stress lay from this point of view on the *handfasting*, the *giftermål*, the symbolic purchase or the agreement to marry: the Popes, speaking for the Church, did not consider such promises *de futuro* as decisive. On the other hand the promise *de presenti*, even apart from any ecclesiastical ceremony, was protected as a sacramental act.[8]

The general result is expressed in the decretals of Gregory IX. The only absolutely indissoluble marriage was the *matrimonium consummatum*. A *matrimonium non consummatum* might be voidable, but only through the action of the Pope; the parties could not break it off except in the single case of either of them wanting to enter "religion". What Alexander III then had done was to introduce the direct action of the Papacy as the sole judge of doubtful marriages.

Sacrament created an indissoluble tie in Canon Law, but in the practice of the secular world innumerable cases arose in which the continuance of marital relations was found to be impossible. The Roman Church tried to avoid these difficulties by casuistic devices to assist people in annulling marriages on some pretext or other instead of divorcing the spouses. In these devices and in the power to withhold dispensation it constantly came into conflict with secular opinions and secular powers.

In order to extend as far as possible the domain of ordered family life the Church purified illegitimate unions by means of subsequent matrimony and regarded the offsprings of such unions as legitimate children. In this respect it came into conflict with the

---

8. A. L. SMITH, *Church and State in the Middle Age*, pp. 71-2.

interests and customary practice of feudal lords, of whom certainty as regards legitimacy was an important feature in the treatment of succession. Hence the famous refusal of the barons of England in the conference of Merton (1236) to accept the Ecclesiastical view of legitimation *per subsequens matrimonium*. Nolumus leges Angliae mutari. The decided stand of the English magnates on this occasion by no means proves that the Church lost her cause for ever. The proceedings as to legitimacy remained complicated and continued to give rise to constant dispute between Courts Christian and Courts of Common Law. The Popes did not give up their intention, but steered a straight course or a casuistic one according to circumstances.[9] This may serve as an example of the interference of the Roman Curia in social arrangements. Whatever the concessions and compromises made in practice, the Church relied in a general way on Christian doctrines as to sources of law which were not contested by the laity and served as a powerful weapon in vindicating the rights of the spiritual power.

To begin with there was the general proposition that positive law as it is shown in statutes, decrees, Royal statements of custom, professional declarations, Acts of Parliament, etc., is of less authority than the Divine Law contained in the revealed teaching of the Church and the Law of Nature implanted by Providence in the soul of man.[10]

The law of nature is discoverable not only in the general propositions and dogmas of human reason, but also in the positive laws themselves in as far as they testify to universal and concordant views. Such a concordance of laws of various national origin constitutes the *jus gentium*.

Now there are two kinds of authorities from which the contents of the common law of nature and of nations can be ascertained:

---

9. Cf. POLLOCK AND MAITLAND, *History of English Law*.
10. THOMAS AQUINAS, *Commentary to Aristotle, Eth. Nic.* v, 10: Attenditur autem in homine duplex natura. Una quidem, secundum quod est animal, quae sibi et aliis animalibus est communis. Alia autem natura est hominis, prout scilicet secundum rationem discernit turpe et honestum.

the civil law, formulated by Rome, and the canon law proclaimed by the Church. Both are recognized by mediaeval schoolmen, but in spite of this affinity, there are fundamental differences between them; there must be a power invested with decision, and this power is found by the schoolmen in the pronouncements of the vicars of Christ — the Popes.

The edifice of Papal justice, like all other forms of judicature, needed material guarantees of compulsion, and it stood erect as long as the principal of these guarantees — the power of excommunication and interdict — kept its authority over Christian society. Its effects were terrible, as we may gather, for instance, from the description of the state of England under the bann of the interdict proclaimed by Innocent III.

It is significant that in the closing centuries of the Middle Ages — the XIV and XV — the foundations of theocracy gave way because material conditions of social life asserted themselves more and more strongly as against mystic aspirations towards the life of a universal church. This is evident in the policy of the Popes themselves — the craving for temporal power in certain provinces, especially in Southern Italy and France, the development of Papal fiscality since Innocent IV. But it is even more prominent in the growth of national separatism conditioned by the formation of Western States. Already in Dante's writings the main stress is laid on the necessity of material compulsion, for which he looks, however, to a reconstruction of the Roman Empire. More ominous from the practical point of view is the rise of national unity in the various

---

Juristae autem illud tantum dicunt jus naturale, quod consequitur inclinationem naturae communis homini et aliis animalibus, sicut conjunctio maris et feminae, educatio natorum, et alia hujusmodi. Illud autem jus, quod consequitur propriam inclinationem naturae humanae, scilicet ut homo est rationale animal, vocant juristae jus gentium, quia eo omnes gentes utuntur, sicut quod pacta sint servanda et quod legati sint apud hostes tuti et alia hujusmodi. Utrumque autem horum comprehenditur sub justo naturali, prout hic a Philosopho accipitur.

kingdoms of the West, in the England of Edward III with its strong opposition to appeals to the Curia, in the France of XIV century with its legists brought up on civil law and using it to build up a doctrine of National self-sufficiency.

A characteristic expression of this disruptive movement of political self-assertion is to be found in the work of the leading Commentator of Civil law — Bartolus (1314-1357). He is quite ready to recognize the theoretical unity of European common law, the legal tradition of the Empire and the spiritual superiority of the Pope.[11] We have seen above that Statutes, no less than laws, are subjected to the higher laws — the *jus divinum, jus naturale* and *jus gentium*. Further, statutes which as regards "spiritualia" are contrary to the Canons are of course invalid; and we may note that statutes contrary to the liberties of the Church are similarly invalid, even where Imperial laws seem valid. Now let us consider the general rules to be observed between the conflicting *jura municipalia* and the *jus commune*. In his commentary on the law *Omnes populi* Bartolus asks whether Statutes could vary the rules laid down in the common civil law.[12] He answers that a statute cannot contradict the *jus commune* by ordaining that which the *jus commune* forbids; but it can ordain that which is not expressly forbidden, provided that it accords with *boni mores* and public utility, and is within the limits of the jurisdiction which the people can exercise.

Under cover of theoretical deductions Bartolus builds up a legal order of *de facto* institutions based on the actual existence of a number of independent cities capable of establishing their own governments and laws.[13]

From the point of view of public international law the advent of the *Regna* and *Civitates* meant a disruption of the mediaeval society of Christendom. But it meant also the necessity of providing

---

11. WOOLF, *Bartolus of Sassoferrato*, pp. 149-151.
12. "An super his, quae disposita vel prohibita sunt a jure civili communi possint fieri statuta aliter statuendo".
13. SIDNEY WOOLF, *Bartolus of Sassoferrato*, p. 388.

by conventions and alliances for the regulation of commercial and intellectual intercourse. For a time Italy seemed to have kept in substance to the conditions and doctrines of the Conflict of Laws initiated by ancient Greek Commonwealths. But lawyers brought up on a study of the *Corpus Juris* treated the matter of private international law in a systematic and closely reasoned form. It is therefore no exaggeration to say that we owe to Bartolus the first and fundamental treatise on the Conflict of Laws. I will just refer to the first sentences of the Bartolus Commentary on the first and second part of the Code in Professor Beale's translation in order to give you an idea of the manner in which the subject was discussed by the great Italian jurist.[14]

"I. Now let us come to the gloss which says "if a Bolognian makes a contract at Modena, he shall be judged by the Statute of Modena". As to this, two things are to be noted: first, whether a statute extends beyond its territory to those not subject; second, whether the effect of a statute extends beyond the territory of the legislator. And first, I ask, what about contracts? Suppose a contract celebrated by a foreigner in this city: a contest arises, and suit is brought in the place where the contract was made: of what place should the statutes be observed or looked at? We either speak of statute or custom with respect to the form of the contract itself, or the suit on it, or with respect to jurisdiction over the performance provided for in the contract itself etc."

To sum up. One might say that at the close of the middle ages the subconsciousness of individuals, of social groups and of political organisations produced centrifugal forces which made it impossible to sustain Christendom. Instead of looking up to providential guidance and appealing to the Pope as vicar of Christ to settle articles of faith, cases of conscience and international feuds, the peoples of Europe attempted to organize a combination of individuals under the sway of territorial states.

---

14. J. H. BEALE, *Bartolus on the Conflict of Laws*, pp. 17, 18, 19.

V. THE INTERNATIONAL RELATIONS OF TERRITORIAL STATES

The unity of Western Christendom was gradually dissolving in the XIV and XV centuries. Its spiritual and material foundations were giving way before new forces. The barrenness of dialectical scholasticism was discarded in the light of the Revival of learning and of experimental science. A revolt of individual conscience against external discipline brought about the disruption of the Church. Thomas of Aquinas had deduced from scripture the call of the Priests to act as Kings of the people in matters of supreme importance. Luther deduced from it the priestly and Kingly office of plain Christians! He wrote in his first revolutionary pamphlet "the Freedom of the Christian" (1521):

"Who is able to express the freedom and highness of Christian man? Through his Kingship he has power over all things, through his priesthood he has power over God, because God complies with his prayer and will, as it is written in the Psalter: "God acts in accordance with the will of those who fear him, and listens to their prayer". And the Christian wins this honour exclusively through faith, not by any works. From this it can be seen that a Christian is free of all things and above all things, so that he has no need of good works in order to be pious and blessed, faith brings him everything in plenty. And should he be so foolish as to think that he can become pious, true, blessed or a Christian by good works, he would lose faith with all things, like the dog which carried a piece of meat in his mouth and snapped after the reflection in the water: he lost both the meat and the reflection."

In the economic sphere feudal relations based on natural husbandry were being replaced by commercial intercourse on a large scale. Politically modern states were growing up on a territorial basis, welded together sometimes by national consciousness as in France and Great Britain, sometimes by provincial and municipal competition as in Italy and Germany, but everywhere under the guidance of selfassertive and unscrupulous sovereigns; guided by State selfishness (*raison d'état*). No wonder the old conception of

Christian Commonwealth (*Respublica Christiana*) had to be abandoned and the Catholic unity was broken up by a disruptive Reformation. The question was, what principle would take the place of this shattered "Universality."[1]

It seemed at first that the victory had been definitely won by the territorial principle. If universal order was given up territorial peace had to take its place: it was attainable by the creation of strong and uncontested authority. The *Defensor Pacis* of Marsilius of Padua presented an early justification of the secular system of polities.[2] Macchiavelli in *The Prince* described the means, fair and foul, by which domination could be attained and maintained.

After the terrible religious feuds of the XVIth and XVIIth centuries the demand for civil peace asserted itself with particular force in the kingdom of Henry IV of France and in the English Restoration. I need hardly remind you that the modern theory of sovereignty may be traced to the writings of Bodin, who was, as it were, obsessed by the idea that the only means of preventing endless and destructive strife is to admit the final decision of an uncontested monarchical authority in the State. Hobbes gave an even more pungent expression to the craving for civil peace. Religious conviction itself was subordinated by him to the

---

1. See J. N. FIGGIS, *From Gerson to Grotius*.
2. *Defensor Pacis*, c. 12. Nos autem dicamus secundum veritatem atque consilium Aristotelis, 3 politicae, ca. 6, legis latorem, seu causam legis effectivam primam et propriam, esse populism, seu civium universitatem aut eius valentiorem partem, per suam electionem sen voluntatem in generali civium congregatione per sermonem expressam, praecipientem seu determinantem aliquid fieri seu omitti circa civilis actus humanos sub poena vel supplicio temporali: valentiorem, iniquam partem, considerata quantitate in communitate illa super quam lex fertur, sive id fecerit universitas praedicta civium aut eius pars valentior per se ipsam immediate, sive id alicui vel aliquibus commiserit faciendum... Et dico consequenter huic quod eadem auctoritate prima non alia debent leges et aliud quod libet per electionem institutum approbationem necessariam suscipere, &c....

paramount craving for authority and the modern "Cuius regio, ejus religio" was not only the decision of the Augsburg Diet.

And yet one has to look deeper in order to understand the course of events. The subjection of religion to secular authority was after all a lame expedient. State Sovereignty in its theoretical completeness as formulated by Hobbes amounted to a mechanical compression of individual atoms. The State Leviathan assumed the appearance of a monstrous organism, but it was conceived as a mechanical contrivance. The force of Hobbes' argument depended on the fact that he had simplified the political problems to the utmost by reducing them to two factors — separate individuals, incapable of creating society, and the State, a "persona ficta", through whose compulsion the intercourse between isolated individuals became possible, but which was in truth the creation of individual brains. The atomism of individuals, disconnected in nature and connected by mechanical coercion, is the general principle in which both extremes are united. Spinoza's *Tractatus Theologico-politicus* presented a variation of the same reasoning.

Although there was ample justification in these doctrines for the policy of King's Craft projected by a James I and practised by a Frederic II, it would be impossible to disregard the fact that the glorification of territorial sovereignty never succeeded in silencing the claims of citizens to an altogether different standing — to a political existence in their own right on the strength of the inherent dignity and self-conciousness of human nature. As against the State despotism of the time rose the monarchomachi, the enemies of Kings, on the one hand, the Jesuits, the satellites of a religious society, on the other. In public law these extremes actually met: both justified revolution and the assassination of tyrants. But it is more important to notice that these two schools, opposed to the absolutism of the territorial State, worked together to prepare the ground for the most characteristic doctrine of this time — the conception of a law of Nature as a guidance for the relations between states.

The conception of a supreme Law of Nature is, of course, not a product of modern times. The view that laws are derived in the end from natural reason was a constant topic of argument among Greek philosophers and the doctrine of a law of Nature became one of the main tenets of the Stoic teaching. Mediaeval schoolmen adopted it from Aristotle's writings as well as from Scripture and from the Fathers. But while in these earlier epochs the admission of natural law as one of the forces of political life and jurisprudence was balanced and modified by other equally powerful principles, e. g. by the absorbing influence of the City Commonwealth, of the Empire, theocratic commandments, in the period starting with the Reformation it became the very foundation of social justice. The roots of law had to be sought in the nature of man, as the roots of religion were found in the personal relation between man and Providence. A powerful school of thought culminating in Grotius' work declined to consider human relations as productions of selfishness and successful violence: it took its stand against Macchiavelli and Hobbes on a social attraction engrained in human nature.

The age with its rationalistic frame of thought was intent on discovering *axiomatic truths* from which the various details of natural science and social doctrine could be deduced with strict consistency. And jurists and theologians looked for these axiomatic truths in a law of nature.

This is how Grotius explains the position:

"In the first place it was my object to refer the truth of the things which belong to Natural law to some notions, so certain, that no one can deny them, without doing violence to his own nature. For the principles of such Natural Law, if you attend to them rightly, are of themselves patent and evident, almost in the same way as things which are perceived by the external senses . . . . "[3]

---

3. GROTIUS, *De jure belli et pacis*, trans. by W. WHEWELL, Cambridge 1853. *Prolegomena*, 39. Primum mihi cura haec fuit, ut eorum quae ad jus naturae per tinent probationes referrem ad notiones quasdam tam certas, ut eas

I quote them (philosophers, historians, poets and orators) as witnesses whose conspiring testimony, proceeding from innumerable different times and places, must be referred to some universal cause; which, in the questions with which we are here concerned, can be no other than a right deduction proceeding from the principles of reason, or some common consent. The former cause of agreement points to the Law of Nature, the latter to the Law of Nations: though the difference of these two is not to be collected from the testimonies themselves, (for writers everywhere confound the Law of Nature and the Law of Nations), but from the quality of the matter. For what cannot be deduced from certain principles by solid reasoning, and yet is seen and observed everywhere, must have its origin from the will and consent of all."

"Natural Law is so immutable that it cannot be changed by God himself. For though the power of God be immense, there are some things to which it does not extend: because if we speak of those things being done, the words are mere words, and have no meaning, being selfcontradictory. Thus God himself cannot make twice two not be four; and in like manner, he cannot make that which is intrinsically bad, not be bad."[4]

---

nemo negare possit, nisi sibi vim inferat. Principia enim ejus juris, si modo animum recte advertas, per se patent atque evidentia sunt, ferme ad modum eorum quae sensibus externis percipimus.

40. ... ubi multi diversis temporibus ac locis idem pro certo affirmant, id ad causam universalem referri debeat: quae nostris quaestionibus alia esse non potest, quam aut recta illatio ex naturae brincipiis procedentes, aut communis aliquis consensus. Illa jus naturae indicat, hic jus gentium: quorum discrimen non quidem ex ipsis testimoniis, (passim enim scriptores voces juris naturae et gentium permiscent) sed ex materiae qualitate intelligendum est. Quod enim ex certis principiis certa argumentatione deduci non potest, et tamen ubique observatum apparet, sequitur ut ex voluntate libera ortum habeat.

4. *Ibid.* i, I, x. 5. Est autem jus naturale adeo immutabile, ut ne a Deo quidem mutari queat. Quanquam enim immensa est Dei potentia, dici

Suarez explains the relation between the various kinds of law in the following way:[5] "The reason for the existence of this kind of law consists in the fact that mankind, though divided into a variety of nations and kingdoms, belongs to a "universitas" of some sort, not only in the special sense of the word, but in a quasi-political and moral sense. This is indicated by the natural precept of reciprocal love and pity which is extended to all, even to foreigners of any nation. Thus, while every Commonwealth or kingdom presents a perfect community in itself, nevertheless each is at the same time a member of the universe in as much as it concerns mankind. Because none of these communities is so selfsufficient as to be independent of reciprocal help, association and intercourse. Sometimes this is

---

tamen quaedam possunt, ad quae se illa non extendit. Sicut ergo ut bis duo non sint quatuor ne a Deo quidem potest effici, ita ne hoc quidem, ut quod intrinseca ratione malum est, malum non sit.
5. F. SUAREZ, *Tractatus de legibus ac Deo Legislatore*, London, 1679. II, C. 19 § 9, Ratio autem ejus partis, & juris est, quia humanum genus quantumvis in yarios populos et regna divisum, semper habet aliquam unitatem non solum specificam, sed etiam quasi politicam, & moralem, quam indicat naturale praeceptum mutui amoris, & misericordiae, quod ad omnes extenditur, etiam extraneos, & cujuscumque rationis. Quapropter licet unaquaeque civitas perfecta, respublica, aut regnum, sit in se communitas perfecta, ac suis membris constans numquam enim illae communitates adeo sunt sibi sufficientes singillatim, quin indigeant aliquo mutuo juvamine, & societate, ac communicatione, interdum ad melius esse, majoremque utilitatem; interdum vero etiam ad moralem necessitatem, & indigentiam, ut ex ipso uso constat. Hoc ergo ratione indigent aliquo jure, quo dirigantur, & recte ordinantur in hoc genere communicationis, & societatis. Et quamvis magna ex parte hoc fiat per rationem naturalem; non tamen sufficienter, & immediate quod omnia; ideoque aliqua specialia jura potuerunt usu earundem gentium introduci. Nam sicut in una civitate, vel provincia consuetudo introducit jus, ita in universo humano genere, potuerunt jura gentium moribus introduci. Eo vel maxime, quod ea, quae ad hoc jus pertinent, et pauca sunt, & juri naturali valde propinqua, & que facillimam habent ab jib deductionem.

desirable for the sake of a better existence and greater usefulness, sometimes on account of moral needs and indigence, revealed by practice. For this reason they require a certain kind of law to direct and to place them in order in this kind of intercourse. And although this is achieved to a great extent by natural reason, the latter does not suffice. Therefore certain special forms of law have been actually introduced. As in every single city or province custom creates legal rules, in the same way as regards mankind laws of nations may be introduced by moral usage. This is easy because rules of that kind are not many and are closely akin to the law of nature from which they can be derived without difficulty."

On the other side, Althusius, a German professor who taught in East Friesland and was strongly influenced by the thought and life of the Netherlands, built up his politics on a conception of a *Social Compact* distinct from all governmental arrangements, but necessary in order to explain the existence of society formed of a multitude of living individuals.

The speculative position of Althusius marks a new departure in political thought. As in the case of Hobbes and of Rousseau the organization of government is relegated to the background. The main thing is to account for the appearance of society itself. It is assumed that it is rendered possible by two tendencies — a psychological one, the bent of human nature towards social intercourse — the *Socialitas* of Grotius, modified from the ζῶον πολιτικὸν of Aristotle; — and the conscious association of men for purposes of cooperation. It is highly characteristic of the fundamental individualism of the epoch that society is treated as a form of partnership (Societas) rather than as an organic unity.[6]

---

6. OTTO GIERKE, *Johannes Althusius*, Breslau, p. 99. ... Gleich an die Eingangspforte seiner Politik stellt er die Fundamentirung des Gattungsbegriffes "consociatio" auf ausdrhcklichen oder stillschweigenden Konsens der Associirten. Selbst fhr die Familienverbindungen halt er, obschon er sie als nathrliche und nothwendige Verhaltnisse anerkennt, die Fiktion der Vertragsgrundlage aufrecht. Zur vollen Entfaltung aber bringt er den

It would be wrong to suppose, however, that these political doctrines were purely the products of theoretical reflection and study. The theories served as a nucleus to ideas of a practical nature and of intense influence on the life of the people. The connecting link was given by religious struggles of the time in which territorial sovereigns were confronted by unconquerable convictions in faith and creed. In spite of the Diet of Augsburg, of the Westphalian treaties, of the *raison d'état* persecutions of Catherine of Medici and of Louis XIV, the political thought of these times insisted more and more effectively on the rights of man in the religious and, eventually, in the social domain. The significant tradition of the right of man to freedom of thought and action starts from the Puritan opposition to the Stewarts, asserts itself in the colonial constitutions of the new world before reaching its formulas in the Declaration of Independence and of the French revolutionary Declarations.

The struggle for religious autonomy in the XVII century produced actual attempts to construct States on the basis of contract. This is how nineteen emigrants from Providence (Rhode Island) formulated the fundamental law in their new settlement: "We whose names are underwritten do here solemnly in the presence of Jehovah incorporate ourselves into a bodie politick, and as he

---

Vertragsgedanken fhr Korporationen, Gemeinde und Staat, die er durchweg als freiwillig eingegangene, wenn auch durch die gesellige Natur des Menschen bedingte Verhaltnisse auffasset. gberal nimmt er hier einen zu Grunde liegenden formlichen "contractus societatis" an, den er ohne Bedenken den Regeln des Civilrechts unterstellt. Indem er sodann bis ins Einzelne bei jeder Verbandsart den Inhalt der vertragsmassigen Vergemeinschaftung analysirt, gewinnt er die Mittel zu dem bis dahin in dieser Weise niemals unternommenen Versuch einer festen Grenzziehung zwischen den Rechtssphären des Individuums und der Gemeinschaft, sowie der engeren und der weiteren Verbande. Lediglich aus dem Begriff des Gesellschaftsvertrages vollzieht er den Aufbau einer mit allen staatlichen Hoheiitsrechten über ihre Glieder ausgerüsteten Volksgesammtheit, um dann erst hinter her sich dem zwischen ihr und ihren Verwaltern bestehenden Vertragsverhältniss zuzuwenden.

shall help, will submit our persons, lives and estates unto our Lord Jesus Christ, the King of Kings, and Lord of Lords, and to all those perfect and absolute laws of him given us in his holy word of truth, to be guided and judged hereby."[7] In England itself the victorious Puritan army drew up a "project of the agreement of the people" (1657) in which the contractual origin of state organization is clearly stated.

An Agreement of the People of England, and the places therewith incorporated, for a secure and present peace, upon grounds of common right, freedom and safety.

Having, by our late labours and hazards, made it appear to the world at how high a rate we value our just freedom, and God having so far owned our cause as to deliver the enemies thereof into our hands, we do now hold ourselves bound, in mutual duty to each other, to take the best care we can for the future, to avoid both the danger of returning into a slavish condition and the chargeable remedy of another war.[8]

Thus the period which began with the Renaissance and attained its culminating point in the French Revolution is dominated by the struggles and compromises of two principles — that of the natural justice derived from individual consciousness and that of the sovereignty in the territorial state, derived from the requirement of social order. In a world of this kind international relations, when not abandoned to settlement by pure force had to conform also to the fundamental tendencies of the political thought of the times. And we see them indeed built up by the help of conceptions derived from an individualistic law of nature.

The application of the Law of Nature to international relations was conditioned by the view that political life was altogether

---

7. JELLINEK, *Staats-und Völkerrechtl. Abhandlungen*, ii, 36. Agüednek, 1638.
8. S. R. GARDINER, *Constitutional Documents of the Puritan Revolution*, Oxford, 1906, p. 359.

proceeding in two channels a state of voluntary arrangements established by convention and defended by compulsion, and a previous state of Nature in which rights and duties had to be deduced from considerations of human reason and, hence, of natural justice. Gentili and Suarez proclaim in the same way that as relations between states are not regulated by common sovereignty, they must be regulated by principles of natural justice. These principles are more or less clearly recognized by all those who believe in God as the fountain of morality and justice. Those who do not share in this fundamental belief are outlaws in civilized society.[9]

A fundamental rule from which all other positive rules are derived is: *Pacta sunt servanda*. It is the basis of confidence between men, without which no social or international co-operation is possible.

"For in the first place, it follows therefrom that pacts between kings and different peoples, so long as nothing thereof is performed (re integra) have no force; the parties being bound by no common instituted law; especially in those places in which no regular form of treaties and engagements has been introduced. And again, no reason can be found why laws, which are in a certain way a common pact of the people, and are so called by Aristotle and Demosthenes, should be able to give obligatory force to pacts."[10]

---

9. ALBERICUS GENTILIS, *De jure belli*, Oxonii, 1877, I, 9, p. 39. . . . At neque nos loquimur nunc de his qui, ferarum modo magis quam hominum viventes, sine ulla omnino religione sunt; hos enim quasi piratas, communes hostes omnium, bello persequendos, et cogendos in mores hominum arbitrarer.

Cf. J. N. FIGGIS, *Studies of political thought from Gerson to Grotius*, Cambridge, 1907.

10. H. GROTIUS, *De jure belli et pacis*, ii, c. ii, I, 3. Primum enim sequitur inde inter reges et populos diversas, pactorum, quandiu nihil ex iis praestitum est, vim esse nullam, praesertim iis in locis, ubi nulla certa forma foederum aut sponsionum reperta est. Tum vero ratio nulla reperiri potest, cur leges, quae quasi pactum commune sunt populi, atque hoc nomine vocantur ab Aristotele et Demosthene, obligationem pactis possint addere.

HISTORICAL TYPES OF INTERNATIONAL LAW   123

The framework of a law of nature is thus fundamental for the international jurisprudence of the XVII and XVIII centuries.

"By many the law of nature and the law of nations are held to be one and the same, differing merely in outward name. Hence Hobbes (*De Cive*, c. 14, 4, 5) divides natural law into natural law of persons... and natural law of States, which latter is commonly called the law of nations. The rules of both', he adds, 'are the same'.... With this opinion we certainly agree."[11]

Does this mean that all the speculations of these times were doomed to be phantastical or Utopian, a dream of students or a screen for cynical greed? In practice, undoubtedly, diplomatic arguments have been often conducted in a spirit of scarcely disguised selfishness. Frederic II of Prussia began his career as a political thinker by writing a treatise called "Anti-Macchiavel." And neither he, nor Joseph II, nor Catherine II, escaped from the influence of the ideas of natural law in certain respects. Take, for example, the policy of letting everyone achieve salvation in his own way— nach seiner "façon," practised by Frederic, or the levelling of social differences decreed by Joseph II; these measures were certainly a considerable advance on the "cujus regio ejus religio" or on the programme of class privileges of Montesquieu.

What is even more important is the fact that a body of international doctrine grew up at the hands of Grotius, of Pufendorf, of Vattel, which formulated rules of international usage, that had considerable authority even with the most arbitrary rulers. It may be idle to talk in this case about *law* (lex), as we are accustomed to give this name to compulsory rules, but it is quite appropriate to talk about natural justice, because these conceptions imply

---

11. S. PUFFENDORF, *De jure naturae et gentium*, Amsterdam, 1688. II, c. 3, 23. ...Multis jus naturae & jus gentium in se unum & idem habetur, quod extrinseca duntaxat denominatione differat. Inde & HOBBES, de Cive, c. 14, 4, 5 naturalem legem dividit "in naturalem hominum, ... naturalem civitatum, quae vulgo jus gentium adpellatur. Praecepta utriusque, addit, eadem sunt. . ."

the formulation and declaration of rights even apart from actual decision and execution. And there is no reason why this quality of principles orientated towards equity and justice should be denied to international jurisprudence. As a matter of fact while we reject nowadays the *a priori* assumptions of an immutable law of nature, we recognize the value of public opinion as to the equitable regulation of international affairs; while treatment of "peace" by international law is governed by such public opinion and by definite agreements in which considerations of common utility and equity play a decisive part. In this light the earlier teaching of the law of nature becomes important and suggestive.

Those who examine its particulars, find, to begin with, that it transfers to States the juridical ideas and requirements worked out by earlier generations in the domain of private law. Once States are conceived as persons on a footing of equality brought together under the protection of incontested sovereignty their collective life is treated as that of normal persons in private law; they enter into transactions, assume responsibilities, conclude conventions, make claims, demand compensations, commit delicts. In this latter respect the international doctrine of Grotius and Gentili assumed a distinctly realistic aspect. A State could not plead immunity from accusation in fact on the ground that it is merely a fiction and that "*Universitas non delinquit.*" Being organized under a government it incurs all the consequences of its deliberate acts although these consequences may be drawn not by a superior tribunal but by self-help under natural law. This is the reason and justification of war. This view gives rise to the following interesting argument: "And so far we follow the opinion of Innocentius, and of others who say that war may be made against those who sin against nature; contrary to the tenets of Victoria, Vasquius, Azolius, Molina, and others; who seem to require, in order to justify a war, that he who undertakes it should be either injured in his own person, or in the country to which he belongs, or that he should have jurisdiction over him whom he attacks. For they hold that the power of punishing is the proper effect of Civil Jurisdiction; while we conceive that it comes also from Natural Law. If the opinion of those from whom we dissent be admitted, an enemy will not have the power of punishing an enemy, even after war has been justly begun, if it be for another cause than to inflict punishment: which right, however, most authors concede, and the usage of all nations confirms, not only after the war has been finished, but even while it is going on; and this right is claimed, not from any civil jurisdiction, but from that natural right which existed before states existed, and is still in force in places in which men live distributed into families and not into states."[12]

Another example of the application of the private law conceptions of personality to States is the recognition of their equality before the law; England and Portugal remained equal even when Portugal ceased to be a great power either at home or in the colonies, and we know of many more striking examples of international equality nowadays. The point is not a negligible one, of course, because it conditions the whole practice of international conferences and joint decisions.

Another aspect of the transfer of private law conceptions into the domain of international law is the influence of Roman jurisprudence in shaping the principal doctrines of the latter.[13]

---

12. GROTIUS, *De Jure belli et pacis* ii, c. xx, § 40, 4.
Et eatenus sententiam sequimur Innocentii, et aliorum qui beilo aiunt peti posse eos qui in naturam delinquunt: contra quam sentiunt Victoria, Vasquius, Azolius, Molina, aiii, qui ad justitiam belli requirere videntur, ut qui suscipit aut laesus sit in se aut republica sua, aut ut in eum qui bello impetitur jurisdictionem habeat. Ponunt enim illi puniendi potestatem esse effectum proprium jurisdictionis civilis, cum nos eam sentiamus venire etiam ex jure naturali, qua de re aliquid diximus libri primi initio. Et sane si illorum a quibus dissentimus admittatur sententia, jam hostis in hostem puniendi jus non habebit, etiam post juste susceptum bellum ex causa non punitiva: quod tamen jus plerique concedunt et usus omnium Gentium confirmat, non tantum postquam debellatum est, sed et manente bello; non ex ulla jurisdictione civili, sed ex illo jure naturali quod et ante institutas civitates fuit, at nunc etiam viget, quibus in locis homines vivunt in familias non in civitates distributi.
13. Albericus GENTILIS, *De jure belli*, i, c. 3, (p. 16). . . . Jus etiam, illis perscriptum libris Justiniani, non civitatis est tantum, sed et gentium,

Indeed, no better illustration of this method could be given than the one presented by the text of Grotius' famous and epoch-making works. To take only one instance. The cardinal doctrine of occupation is inspired by well known precepts of Roman Law. The concrete cases which presented themselves for discussion and settlement were chiefly suggested by the policy of discoverers, colonizers and traders. The reaction against vague claims of ineffective accusations by the Portuguese and the Spaniards, the disputes as to the assertion of sovereignty in narrow seas and territorial waters exercised the civil law learning of Dutch and English jurists and led up to the formulation of views which have been found useful in such events as the Berlin conference of 1885 on the attribution of possessions and of spheres of influence in Africa.

The weak side of public international law — the absence of compulsory sanctions was, of course, evident from the first, and could not be removed by a jurisprudence which had renounced the conception of a theocratic Super-State and pinned its faith to the idea of territorial sovereignty. As has been said already, it was bound

et naturae, et aptatum sic est ad naturam universum, ut imperio extincto, et ipsum ius diu sepultum surrexerit tamen, et in omnes se effuderit gentes humanas. Ergo et Principibus stat: etsi privatis conditum a Justiniano. Et stat sane nec auditum mihi est, lectumve unquam, quod egregii illi supra vulgum positi tradunt. Forte an desiit esse gentium, et naturae ius, quia expositum est civitati? Sed ut qnod civile est, non idem continuo est gentium: quod tamen gentium est, idem et civile esse debet. Est quidem ius civile, quod non servit naturali, et gentium juri per omnia: at neqne in totum a naturali recedit, vel gentium. Et cura non serviat per omnia, aut ratio communis omnium civitatum facit, aut singularis aliquarum. Ut quod civilia jura non omne agnoscant pactum ad actionem, cum gentium jus differentiam pactorum nullam constituat. .. Caeterum si quid eiusmodi proprium civitatis non ostenditur, illud de his tollere publicarum rerum disceptationibus plusquam ridiculum fuerit, plusquam ineptum. Quid? Non apta Principibus illa librorum Justiniani, Honeste vivere, Alterum non laedere, Suum cuique tribuere, Liberos tueri, Injuriam propulsare, Cum omnibus hominibus cognationem agnoscere, Commercia retinere.. .? Isthaec juris gentium sunt, et juris beilici.

to recognize war as the natural outcome of self-help and its civilising influence was directed towards preventing wanton atrocities and mitigating inevitable horrors. How little could be attempted at this stage by the best international jurists may be gathered from the admission of Grotius.[14] In strict law a belligerent was entitled to slaughter the inhabitants of an enemy country, even women and children, and the only restriction to the exercize of this "right" was to be sought in pity and in mercy, not in law.

Such statements were the outcome of a consistent application of the view that a sovereign state is judge of its own case and is not subject to any legal superior. But how was this to be reconciled in practice with the teaching as to natural justice? If the recognition of such justice was to be a mainstay of international jurisprudence, some attempt had to be made to remove the opposition between justice as law and justice as a principle of morals.

---

14. GROTIUS, *De Jure belli et pacis*, iii, c. 4 §§ 8, 9 (WHEWELL, iii, p. 80.)

VI. MODERN DEVELOPMENTS

One of the least contestable generalizations as regards the history of human institutions seems to be that any political principle which governs them tends to push its consequences into extremes and to manifest sooner or later certain harmful tendencies. Aristotle in his teaching on the *via media* as the path to virtue and success, Hegel in his doctrine on the dialectical sequence of position, opposition and composition have drawn attention to various aspects of this law of evolution. An excellent example of its operation in actual life may be supplied by the history of the territorial state. Based on the fundamental idea of sovereignty for the sake of peace it has proved in practice the most powerful agent for establishing sovereignty by international wars. La Bruyère in his famous "Characters" composed in the reign of Louis XIV, reflected sarcastically on the absurdities of Civilisation as manifested in these conflicts.[1]

---

1. LA BRUYÈRE, "Caractères", ed. par CH. LOUANDRE, Paris, 1862, p. 316 ("Des jugements").
..."Que si l'on vous disoit que tous les chats d'un grand pays se sont assemblés par milliers dans une plaine, et qu'après avoir miaulé tout leur soûl, ils se sont jetés avec fureur les uns sur les autres et ont joué ensemble de la dent et de la griffe; que de cette melée il est demeuré de part et d'autre neuf mille chats sur place qui ont infecté l'air à dix lieues de là par leur puanteur, ne diriez vous pas: Voila le plus abominable sabbat dont on ait jamais ouï parler. Et si les loups en faisoient de même, quels hurlements, quelle boucherie!
...Mais, comme vous devenez d'année et d'autre plus raisonnable, vous avez bien enchéri sur cette vielle manière de vous exterminer: vous avez des petits globes qui vous tuent tout d'un coup, s'ils peuvent seulement vous atteindre à la tête ou à la poitrine; vous en avuz d'autres plus pesants et plus massifs, qui vous coupent en deux parts ou qui vous éventrent, sans compter ceux qui, tombaut sur vos toits, enfoncent les planchers, vont du grenier à la cave, en enlèvent les voûtes et font sauter en l'air avec vos maisons vos femmes qui sont en couche, l'enfant et la nourrice.

"If you were told that all the cats of a certain country had assembled in thousands in a plain and after having miauwed to their hearts' content, had attacked each other with rage, with tooth and nail, and that as a result of this struggle nine thousand cats were left dead on the field, infecting the air with the stench of their rotting bodies ten miles around, would you not say: this is the most abominable rumpus that has ever been heard of...

But as you are growing more clever every year, you have introduced great improvements upon this mode of exterminating one another. You possess little balls which kill one outright if they hit head or chest. You have also larger and heavier balls which cut one in two or dismember one, not to mention the fact that in falling on the roof of a house they crash through floors from garret to cellar, break up vaults and hurl into the air together with the houses your wives in childbed and your babies."

In our time we might supplement this ironical picture by much more bitter observations. What we are concerned in, however, is to trace the spiritual reaction against these terrible evils connected with the unlimited freedom of action of territorial sovereigns. After each flood of blood and destruction which marked a stage of European history some attempt was made to find a remedy against the recurrence of the disaster. At the close of the religious wars of the XVI century, the Protestant King who had consented to attend mass in order to pacify France is said to have discussed a magnificent proposal for the establishment of peace in Europe. The fatal drawback of such a plan was that it hinged on the dismemberment of the overwhelming power of the Hapsburgs of Spain and of the Empire, and even Henry IV himself does not seem to have been by any means prepared to renounce territorial acquisitions.[2]

---

2. The narrative as to the conversations between the King and his chief adviser, Sully, was probably put together at a much later date and cannot be regarded as a piece of accurate evidence, but I cannot believe that it was a downright invention.

The Thirty Years war culminating in the peace of Westphalia produced as one of its consequences the monumental work of your great Hugo Grotius, a work in which the recourse to inter national arbitration was clearly indicated as the chief means for preventing international wars.[3]

The close of the reign of the "Great King", Louis XIV, with the misery brought on his country by the succession of his wars with the Empire, England and the Netherlands, has been depicted in vivid colours by one of his most brilliant military chiefs, Marshal Vauban. These wars produced a pacifist manifestation in the memoir of the Abbé de Saint Pierre published in French in 1713, and in English in 1714, just before the peace of Utrecht. The author, the Abbé de St. Pierre, had not only observed the terrible effects of the warlike career of Louis XIV as a spectator; he had been engaged in a minor office in the elaboration of the treaty of Utrecht. He was animated by a fanatical conviction which made him blind to all considerations except those connected with the ideal of pacification. He pronounced a characteristic anathema in regard to all the useless blandishments of science, literature and art, which reminds us of Tolstoy's pronouncements: Colbert lui-même n'échappe pas a ces critiques pour avoir créé l'Académie des Beaux-Arts. A quoi servent la peinture, la sculpture, la musique, la Poésie, la comédie, l'architecture? A prouver le nombre des fainéants, leur goût pour la fainéantise qui suffit à entretenir et à nourrir d'autres espèces de fainéants qui ce piquent d'esprit agréable, mais non pas d'esprit utile; qui veulent exceller sur leurs pareils et se contentent seulement d'exceller dans les bagatelles. Aussi, "Colbert, grand travailleur, en

---

3. DE SAINT PIERRE, *A Project for Settling an Everlasting Peace in Europe*, London, 1714, has for Motto on his title page a quotation from "GROTIUS' De jure belli et acis" Lib. II, c. 23. "Et tum ob hanc, tum ob alias causas utile esset, immo quodammodo factu necessarium, conventus quosdam haberi Christianarum Potestatum, ubi, per eos quorum res non interest, aliorum controversiae definiantur immo... rationes ineantur cogendi partes ut aequis legibus pacem accipiant."

négligeant les compagnies de commerce maritime pour avoir plus de soin des sciences curieuses et des beaux-arts, n'a pas fait autre chose que de prendre l'ombre pour le corps. Il donna l'ombre aux Francais et laissa le corps aux Hollandais et aux Anglais."[4]

The futility of military conflicts and of the attempts to establish a balance of power between the competing States is strongly insisted upon.

The only means to escape from ever recurring and fruitless bloodshed is to agree on a League of Peace between the leading Christian powers and to negotiate agreements even with heathen States like Turkey. The League is to consist eventually of twenty-four allied states or groups of minor states, each of the members having one vote in the Senate of the Confederation. International conflicts, instead of being fought out by war, should be submitted to the League for compulsory arbitration. All the members should contribute to form a coalition Army for carrying out the decisions of the Union in case of resistance or infringement by any party. While contributions in money should be assessed in proportion to the financial means of the various countries, each of the members should send an equal contingent to the common army. The weaker countries should complete the deficiencies in the numbers of their soldiers by mercenary levies salaried with the help of the more wealthy and powerful States. The acknowledged model for this system was found by St. Pierre in the military and fiscal organization of the old German Empire: what was possible in that case seemed to the pacifist writer likely to prove effective in the case of the Christian world.

A characteristic feature of the project consisted in the fact that it aimed exclusively at establishing a permanent *status quo* in home and foreign affairs. The monarchical and republican institutions have each their advantages and their drawbacks.

---

4. J. DROUET, *Annales politiques* (1912). Introd. p. xvii.

De Saint Pierre[5] writes:

...The Monarchick State has one Advantage, namely that in thirty years it may reach a Degree of perfection in its establishments, which a Republick cannot reach in less than a hundred and fifty years, and this proceeds from two Sources; the first, because the Monarch is to have almost all the Honour of a great Enterprize, of a noble Establishment, of a good Government, and this is a great spur to prick him on to act with vigour and Constancy. The second, because the Opinions of the Monarch are never contradicted, neither in the Resolution, nor in the Execution; whereas in Republicks the Honour of an Enterprize is divided among so many Members, that that Spur becomes very weak in each of them; and besides, there, an Opinion, however good or useful it may be, is liable to be contradicted with Authority, either in the Resolution or in the Execution, and that Contradiction stops all its good Effects; but then the Republican State has another Advantage; namely, that when a good Establishment is once formed in it, it is much more durable than in Monarchies.

This being so let every country have and keep its own without change, but not without interference. On the contrary the success of the scheme depends on a pressure to be exerted by the Union not only with the view of stabilizing frontiers and external possessions, but also constitutions and governments. Otherwise disturbances arising within the boundaries of one state are likely to spread to other states and eventually to produce war.

St. Pierre continues:[6]

Article II. The European Society shall not at all concern itself about the Government of any State, unless it be to preserve the Fundamental Form of it, and give speedy and sufficient Assistance to the Princes in Monarchies, and to the Magistrates in Republicks, against any that are Seditious and Rebellious. Thus it will be a Guarantee that the Hereditary Sovereignties shall remain hereditary,

---

5. SAINT PIERRE, *A Project for Settling an Everlasting Peace*, p. 107.
6. Op. cit., p. 108.

according to the Manner and Custom of each Nation; that those that are elective shall remain elective in the Country where Election is usual; that among the Nations where there are Capitulations, or Conventions which are called *Pacta Conventa*, those sorts of Treaties shall be exactly observed, and that those who in Monarchies should have taken up Arms against the Prince, or in Republicks against some of the chief Magistrates, shall be punished with Death, and Confiscation of Goods.

Explication. The principal Effect of the Union is to preserve all things in Repose in the Condition it finds them in, and as they are the Sovereigns themselves, who, by their Deputies, decide all things in it, they cannot fear that Assembly, any more than each Sovereign can fear himself.

I know it is impossible, especially in Republicks, but that there should be Disputes about Religion, and that as Men never dispute but upon obscure Matters, uncapable of Demonstration, it is impossible to reconcile the two Disputants: But it is possible, it is even easy, for the Magistrates to hinder those Disputes from getting such a Head as to disturb the Tranquility of the State. It is enough at first to impose Silence upon All, and either to banish or imprison those who shall either have spoken, or preached, or written, or printed since the Prohibition. Time discovers the Truth; therefore all that is to be done, till she shews herself clearly to us, is to keep the Subjects from Divisions and from the other Evils that Obscurity may cause to them; and this is what the Prudence and Authority of the Union will always infallibly do in every State of Europe. To keep up the Society, it is not absolutely necessary that the Citizens be of the same Opinion in obscure Matters; nay it is so far from being in their Power, that Uniformity of Opinion upon such Occasions is as it were impossible: But the only Foundation of the Society, is Peace among the Citizens. Thus 'tis requisite that each Citizen, in order to preserve the Society, uses Charity and Indulgence even towards those whom he thinks in an Error. This is what is always not only in the Power of the Citizen, but 'tis also the first and most indispensable of his Duties.

Article III. The Union shall employ its whole Strength and Care to hinder, during the Regencies, the Minorities, the weak Reigns of each State, any Prejudice from being done to the Sovereign, either in his Person, or in his Prerogatives, neither by his Subjects, nor by Strangers; and if any Sedition, Revolt, Conspiracy, Suspicion of Poyson, or any other Violence should happen to the Prince, or the Royal Family, the Union, as its Guardian and Protectress born, should send Commissioners into that State, to look into the Truth of the Facts, and shall at the same time send Troops to punish the Guilty according to the Rigour of the Laws.

Explication. It is certain this Article will be punctually executed, since the United Princes will want neither *Power* nor *Will* to do it. As to *Power*, the thing is evident; as to the *Will*, it is no less evident, since they have no greater Interest than to search as carefully as possible into the Crimes which have destroyed so many Princes, and ruined so many Sovereign Houses, Crimes which so nearly concern them, and to punish the Guilty with all the Severity imaginable, in order to save their own Families, by those exemplary Punishments, from the like Misfortunes."

It is easy to discover the reason of this insistence of St. Pierre on the suppression of internal discord: memories of the international struggles between Protestant and Catholic movements originated in one or the other country and spreading to neighbouring states was still vivid in the minds of all publicists.

The practical impossibility of obtaining such a *perpetuum immobile* and its deathlike aspect did not deter our writer. The difficulty of formulating decisions in a congress of disparate states was realized by him to some extent, but he thought that it could be overcome by the requirement of a three fourths majority for important decisions and the requirement of unanimity in case of alterations of the fundamental articles of the pact.

The project of St. Pierre was inspired by the sight of the misery and destruction, and although there is a good deal of idealism in the views of their originator as to the aims and organisation of the league of states, he reckoned to some extent with actual politics, and put faith on positive combinations of data which would result in international equilibrium and international arbitration. The XVIII century, the age of enlightenment, was bound to take up the problem from another point of view. It came to despair of practical statesmanship, of legal tradition, of constituted powers: in its reaction against feudal survivals and arbitrary kingship it turned to philosophic deductions. In the light of reason politics and law assumed a new aspect and appeared ripe for complete reconstruction. International relations presented a particularly fruitful field for exercize of critical reason. All the great teachers of law of that period recognized a "Law of nature," and constructed systems for its application. The end of the century witnessed a titanic attempt to put these theories into practice. Speculations as to permanent peace were especially appropriate in time of universal war. I should like to call your attention to the most remarkable of these speculations — to Kant's treatment of the problem of international peace.

His Law of Nature (*Naturrecht*) is governed by the central conception established by the *Criticism of Practical Reason (praktischen Vernunft*) — the categorical imperative. Man is essentially free and therefore he recognizes only the dictates of a law of freedom. This means that he ought himself to submit to rules which he is willing to extend to others and to proclaim as universal laws. All reasonable law is reciprocal and it requires the virtual and potential consent of free citizens in order to make it just. This is the justification of a social compact based on reason.

"This agreement, called *contractus originarius* or *pactum sociale*, consisting in the joining of all separate and private wills into one people for the sake of a strictly legal legislation, need not have taken place as a fact. Indeed it is impossible to conceive of it as a fact as if it were necessary to produce historical proofs that a nation whose rights and obligations we have inherited has in reality fulfilled such an Act and must have left oral or written evidence of this in order to be bound by a civil constitution. It is only an Idea of the mind, which carries with it an undoubted practical consequence, namely that it obliges every legislator to make such laws as would arise from the exertion of the will of the whole people, each subject of which, who wishes to be a citizen, should be considered as if he had personally taken part in voting the law. This is the touchstone for the legality of every law: Should the latter be of such a kind that the whole people could not possibly approve of it (e. g. if it were decreed that a particular class should rule permanently by inheritance), such a law would not be just. On the other hand if there is a bare possibility that a people might approve of a certain law, even if it were probable that in case the law were submitted actually for the decision of the people it would not be passed by them at a given moment, it would nevertheless be a duty to uphold such a law.[7]

---

7. IMMANUEL KANT'S *Sämmtliche Werke*, herausgegeben von C. HARTENSTEIN, Leipzig, 1867, v. IV, p. 329. ...Allein dieser Vertrag, (contractus originarius oder pactum sociale genannt), als Coalition jedes besondern und Privatwillens in einem Volk zu einem gemeinschaftlichen und öffentlichen Willen (zum Behuf einer bbs rechtlichen Gesetzgebung) ist keinesweges als ein Factum vorauszusetzen nöthig, (ja als ein solches gar nicht moglich); gleichsam als ob allererst aus der Geschichte vorher bewiesen werden müsste, das ein Volk, in dessen Rechte und Verbindlichkeiten wir als Nachkommen getreten sind einmal wirklich einen solchen Actus verrichtet und eine sichere Nachricht oder ein Instrument davon uns mündlich oder schriftlich hinterlassen haben müsse, um sich an eine schon bestehende bürgerliche Verfassung für gebunden zu achten. Sondern es ist eine blosse Idee der Vernunft, die aber ihre unbezweifelte (praktische) Realität hat: nämlich jeden Gesetzgeber zu verbinden, dass er seine Gesetze so gebe, als sic aus dem vereinigten Willen eines ganzen Volks haben entsprungen können, und jeden Unterthan, sofern er Bürger sein will, so anzusehen, als ob zu einein solchen Willen mit zusammengestimmt habe. Denn das ist der Probierstein der Rechtmässigkeit eines jeden offentlichen Gesetzes. Ist namlich dieses so beschaffen, dass ein ganzes Volk unmoglich dazu seine Einstimmung geben könnte, (wie z. B. dass eine gewisse Klasse von Unterthanen erblich den Verzug des Herrenstandes haben sollten), so ist es nicht gerecht; ist es aber nur moglich, dass ein Volk dazu zusammenstimme, so ist es Pflicht, das Gesetz für gerecht zu halten, gesetzt auch, dass das Volk jetzt in einer solchen Lage oder Stimmung seiner. Denkungsart wäre, dass es, wenn es darum befragt wurde, wahrscheinlicher Weise seine Bestimmung verweigern würde.

The state itself is the result of concert, of a social contract between free individuals in which they give up their isolated and unlimited will in order to acquire a guarantee of their freedom on the basis of law. "It would be wrong to say that in the State man has sacrificed part of his inborn external freedom to attain a certain aim. He has in truth given up his wild, lawless freedom entirely for the sake of a lawful dependence, that is in order to resume an undiminished freedom again in a state of law, because such dependence arises out of his own legislative will."[8]

In this way Kant, following Rousseau, starts from individualistic premises to arrive at the idea of an omnipotent, absolute state.

The fatal contradiction which is so clearly traceable in the legal system of the Roman Empire with its contrast between the absolutism of the sovereign and the free intercourse between individuals and which recurred in the theories of the XVII century, asserts itself again with irresistible force.[9]

Kant was aware of the dilemma and sought to temper it by having recourse to Montesquieu's views on the separation of powers which had obtained increased authority through their adoption by the Constitution of the United States of America. He pleads for a representative Republic as the ideal form of government in which the legislative and the executive powers are separated and yet combined as a major and minor premises are distinct and combined in a syllogism.

It is curious to find the official Professor of Philosophy of the East Prussian University of Konigsberg publicly avowing his predilection for a Republican form of government and following

---

8. KANT, ii. ed., vii, p. 134.
...man kann nicht sagen: der Mensch im Staate habe einem Theil seiner Angebornen äusseren Freiheit einem Zwecke aufgeopfert, sondern er hat die wilde gesetzlose Freiheit gänzlich verlassen, urn seine Freiheit überhaupt in einer gesetzlichen Abhängigkeit, d. i. in einem rechtlichen Zustande unvermindert wieder zu finden: weil diese Abhängigkeit aus seinem eigenen gesetzgebenden Willen entspringt.
9. Cf. E. Caird, *The Critical Philosophy of Immanuel Kant*, ii, p. 354).

closely in his views of the State the apostle of the French Jacobinism, Rousseau. It is even more significant that Kant finds in a Republican reconstruction of the world the clue to the solution of the international problem. It is evident for him, to begin with, that in reasoning on relations between states we have to proceed from the fundamental assumptions that states are juridical persons in a state of nature as regards each other.

"As the state of nature between nations, as well as between single men should be abandoned eventually for the sake of a legal state, therefore all rights of nations anterior to that change, as well as all distinctions between mine and thine, can only be provisional and it is only in a League of States, under the régime of a national State, that they can assume a peremptory character and result in a real peace. As, however, a great extension of such a State of Nations, spreading over wide territories comes into existence, its government and the defence of its members is bound to become impossible; the existence side by side of many such bodies would produce a state of war. Thus permanent peace, the highest aim of international law appears indeed as an idea *incapable* of realisation. But the political principles directed towards associations of States approximating gradually and consistently to this aim are not impossible to realize."[10]

---

10. KANT, H. ed., vii, p. 168. ...Da der Naturzustand der Völker ebensowohl, als einzelner Menschen, ein Zustand ist, aus dem man herausgehen soll, urn in einen gesetzlichen zutreten, so ist vor diesem Ereigniss alles Recht der Völker und alles durch den Krieg erwerbliche oder erhaltbare äussere Mein und Dein der Staaten bloss provisorisch, und kann nur in einem allgemeinen Staatenverein (analogisch mit dem, wodurch ein Volk Staat wird), peremtorisch geltend und ein wahrer Friedenzustand werden. Weil aber, bei gar zu grosser Ausdehnung eines solchen Völkerstaats über weite Landstriche, die Regierung desselben, mithin auch die Beschützung eines jeden Gliedes endlich unmöglich werden muss; eine Menge solcher Corporationen aber wiederum einen Kriegzustand herbeiführt; so ist des ewige Friede, (das letzte Ziel des ganzeu Völkerrechts), freilich eine

This being so, a radical reform of international intercourse could be achieved only by the substitution of a world state for the present anarchical condition in the same way as the territorial state was substituted for the state of disorderly conflicts between individuals.

Kant admits that the institution of the World Commonwealth is not practicable at present and that it would meet with many difficulties in any case, but this does not prevent him from considering it as an ideal aim towards which international relations should be steered. If a cosmopolitan Commonwealth is not possible now, a League of States is already within the domain of possibility.

And here we come again across an expression of confidence in regard to the educational influence of the Republican form of government.

"The putting into practice (objective realisation) of this idea of Feudalism which should extend over all States and lead to permanent peace can be made apparent. If by good luck a powerful and enlightened nation is able to constitute itself into a Commonwealth, which by its nature is bound to tend towards permanent peace, it will became a centre for the federal union of other States, so that they will join it and thus safeguard the freedom of States in accordance with the idea of international aw. Such a federation will gradually extend further and further by means of connections of various kinds."[11]

---

unausführbare Idee. Die politischen Grundsätze aber, die darauf abzwecken, nämlich solche Verbindungen der Staaten einzugehen, als zur continuirlichen Annäherung zu demselben dienen, sind es nicht, sondern, so wie diese eine auf der Pflicht, mithin auch auf dem Rechte der Mensehen und Staaten gegrundete Aufgabe ist, allerdings ausführbar.

11. KANT, H. ed., vi, p. 423. ...Die Ausführbarkeit (objective Realität) dieser Idee der Foderalität die sich allmählig über alle Staaten erstrecken soll, und so zum ewigen Frieden hinführt lässt sich darstellen. Denn wenn das Glück es sofügt, dass ein mächtiges und aufgeklärtes Volk sich zu einer Republik, (die ihrer Natur nach zum ewigen Frieden geneigt sein muss), bilden kann, so gibt diese einen Mittelpunkt der foderativen Vereinigung

It is curious to find that by drawing consequences from his theoretical constructions Kant formulated a number of concrete points which have been taken up recently by the League of Nations movement.

...These preliminary articles prescribe that no treaty of peace shall be made with the secret reservation of causes of quarrel, which might furnish material for another war, that no state shall be treated as the patrimony of an individual, or transferred from hand to hand by inheritance or gift; that no public debts shall be contracted with a view of war, or in preparation for it; that no State shall interfere with the constitution or administration of another; that no State shall use in war such means of injuring the enemy as must make impossible that reciprocal trust which is necessary for peaceful relations in the future, and that on this ground all recourse to the weapons of assassination and poisoning shall be proscribed, and at the same time, all breaches of capitulation or attempts to make use of treachery among the enemy. For such means of war, as they destroy all that trust in the enemy, which is based on our common humanity, and which ought to subsist even in war, tend to produce a war of extermination, which could bring about a lasting peace only in the "great churchyard of the human race."[12]

I venture to think that the facts reviewed in these lectures suggest some conclusions in theory as well as in practice. It seems clear that the contents of political and legal evolutions cannot be brought under the rule of universal abstract formulas: the relations between

---

für ander Staaten ab, um sich an sie anzuschliessen, und so den Freiheitzustand der Staaten, gemäss der Idee des Völkerrechts, zu sichern und sich durch mehrere Verbindungen dieser Art nach und nach imnier weiter auszubreiten.
12. EDWARD CAIRD, *The Critical Philosophy of Immanuel Kant*, Glasgow, 1889. v. ii, p. 348.

Law and the State, between communities and their members vary greatly in the course of history and have to be estimated by different standards. The only two universal and permanently fixed points in this respect are the individual as a given real being and society as a necessary real relation. The problem which every age has to solve is to find the appropriate combinations between the two. The range of actual combination is, however, not the haphazard sequence of a cinematograph impression. We have been able to mark certain definite formulas which have governed particular epochs. We have noticed the regulations of intercourse between the many cities of Greece under a system of conflict of Laws and its decay, as a consequence of the narrow basis of civic privilege on which it was built up. The Roman Imperial system was noticed as an attempt to guarantee freedom of contract and of trade by the unification of political authority. Mediaeval theocracy transferred the centre of the World State from the secular Empire to the Church as a mediator between heaven and earth. Modern history starts from a revolt of individual conscience and individual right against the *Civitas Dei* in its terrestrial aspect. Modern society succeeded in suppressing civil strife and ensuring freedom of contract by the agency of sovereign territorial States, but success in this direction was coupled with orgies of external wars which threaten the existence of civilisation. And so men are again anxiously seeking for a way out of a blind alley. It is evident that there is nothing in the essence of political union to bar the way towards a new conception of the State, wider and more just than that of absolute territorial sovereignty. Theoretically sovereignty is nothing else but finality of decision in case of conflict. It is required under all circumstances, because otherwise disputes will have to be settled by brute force. But it can be as well attached to a tribunal of umpires as to a territorial government. When parties play a game they submit to rules, though they do not submit to each other. In the conduct of a complicated game, like cricket, submission to an umpire may be needed, although the umpire is certainly not regarded as a king. Theoretically the road to settlement by a tribunal of international umpires is open. Practically it is obstructed by the strength and bitterness of national, political, class selfishness. It is only by education and painful object lessons that mankind is learning to prefer peaceful arbitration to the trials of strength in war. Kant was right in appealing to the moral duty of every free man to help in this gradual educational approach towards peace. But in order to achieve results we must be particularly careful not to overstrain our forces, nor to demand from our generation what it is not prepared to yield. Neither the World State nor a Federation with commanding power in political disputes is of our time or within sight.

But apart from international conferences for settling disputes by consultation and compromise the jurisdiction of an international court of Justice for the decision of juridical conflicts is beginning to take shape. It is our duty to work for its success.

BIBLIOGRAPHY

TOWARD A BIBLIOGRAPHY OF THE PUBLISHED WORKS OF SIR PAUL VINOGRADOFF

W. E. Butler

A complete bibliography of the publications of Sir Paul Vinogradoff has yet to be achieved. He published widely throughout the world, and many of his publications, especially prior to 1917, appeared both in English or another western language and in Russian, albeit often under different titles. The previous major effort in this direction, by H. A. L. Fisher, was aware of some Russian titles, but far from all. More remains to be done, and we would be grateful to know of omissions and, in particular, foreign translations of Vinogradoff unknown to us.

ABBREVIATIONS

AEL — *Anthropology and Early Law: Selected from the Writings of Paul Vinogradoff, Frederic W. Maitland, Frederick Pollock, Maxime Kovalevsky, Rudolf Huebner, Frederic Seebohm.* Edited by Lawrence Krader. New York/London, Basic Books, Inc., 1966. [vi], 346 p.

CP — *The Collected Papers of Paul Vinogradoff With a Memoir by The Right Hon. H. A. L. Fisher* [ed. Louise Vinogradoff]. (Oxford, The Clarendon Press, 1928). 2 vols. Reprinted: London, Wildy & Sons Ltd., 1963. 2 vols. Reprinted: New York, Gryphon Editions, 1995. 2 vols. (The Legal Classics Library. Intro. Thomas G. Barnes)

RR — *Россия на распутье* [Russia at the Parting of the Ways] (Москва, Издательский дом «Территория будущего», 2008). 576 р.

ЖМНПр — *Журнал Министерства народного просвещения*

LOCATIONS

GDLC	Library of Congress
DLS	Dickinson School of Law, Pennsylvania State University
IHR	Institute for Historical Research, University of London
Литва	Сводный каталог Литвы
LSE	London School of Economics and Political Science, University of London
MH	Harvard University
MH-L	Harvard University Law School Library
МПГУ	Московский Педагогический государственный университет
НБУк	Национальная библиотека Украины им. Вернадского
PSU	Pennsylvania State University
РГБ	Российская государственная библиотека
РНБ	Российская национальная библиотека
SOAS	School of Oriental and African Studies, University of London
UCL	University College London

1876

"Über die Freilassung zu voller Unabhängigkeit in den deutschen Volksrechten", *Forschungen zur deutschen Geschichte*, IX (1876), 599-608.

1877

(transl.), Guizot, F. P. (1787-1874), *История цивилизации в Франции* [History of Civilization in France] (М., Изд. К. Т. Солдатенкова, 1877). 2 vols.

1878

«Новые ученые работы по феодализму в Италии» [New Doctrines on Feudalism in Italy], *ЖМНПр* (November 1878), ч. 200, отд. IV, pp. 17-29.

1879

«Исторические розыскания в итальянских архивах и библиотеках» [Historical Research in Italian Archives and Libraries], *ЖМНПр* (February 1879), ч. 201, отд. IV, pp. 151-159.

1880

«Происхождение феодальных отношений в Лангобардской Италии» [Origin of Feudal Relations in Lombard Italy], *ЖМНПр* (January 1880), ч. 207, отд. II, pp. 136-212; (February 1880), pp. 344-383; (April 1880), ч. 208, pp. 183-218; (August 1880), ч. 210, pp. 217-253; (September 1880), ч. 211, pp. 186-221; (October 1880), pp.

333-368; (November 1880), ч. 212, pp. 131-164; (December 1880), pp. 330-378.
Thesis for which the degree of Magister was conferred.

Происхождение феодальных отношений в Лангобардской Италии [Origin of Feudal Relations in Lombard Italy]. Спб., тип. В. С. Балашева, 1880. 348, 1 стр. [МПГУ, РНБ]

1881

«Феодализм в Италии» [Feudalism in Italy], *Юридический вестник* [Legal Herald], VIII (1881), pp. 547-566.

1883

"Letter on the Hundred Rolls", *Athenaeum*, (22 December 1883), p. 815.
Letter on the Hundred Rolls of the County of Warwick discovered in the Record Office.

«Очерки западноевропейской историографии» [Essays on Western European Historiography], *ЖМНПр*, № 8 (1883), стр. 390-408; № 9, стр. 160-182; № 10, стр. 371-385; № 11, стр. 176-198; № 12, стр. 485-498.

1884

"A Note Book of Bracton", *Athenaeum* (19 July 1884), pp. 81-82.
Reprinted: *CP*, I, 297-302.
This letter disclosed "an epoch-making discovery", drawing attention to a manuscript in The British Museum which contained "a careful and copious collection of cases" for the first twenty-four years of the reign

of Henry III compiled for the use of Henry de Bratton, the most famous English judge of that period. Vinogradoff in due course acquired a copy of *Henrici de Bracton De legibus & consuetudinibus Angliae libri quinq;: in various tractatus distincti, ad diuersorum et vetustissimorum codicum collationem, ingenti cura, nunc primu typis vulgate: quorum quid cuiq; insit, proxima pagina demonstrabit*. London, Apud Richardum Tottellum, 1569. The provenance of owners of this copy, now in MH-L, is: Richard Organ (17th century); Edmund Reeve (17th century); Baron Guildford, Francis North (1673-1729); Gilbert Walmesley (18th century); John Vaillant (d. 1827); Samuel Putnam (1768-1853); William Green (1806-1880); John Lowell (1824-1897); Frederic William Maitland (1850-1906); Sir Paul Vinogradoff (1854-1925); Asa P. French (1860-1935); George Dunn (1864-1912); Henry Newton Ess (1921-2000); Paul H. Silverstone; Herbert Robinson (donor).

«Очерки западноевропейской историографии» [Essays on Western European Historiography], *ЖМНПр*, № 2 (1884), стр. 433-443; № 6, стр. 310-331; № 7, стр. 171-185; № 11, стр. 183-193.
    Continuation and completion of work whose publication commenced in 1883.

1885

"Oxford and Cambridge Through Foreign Spectacles", *The Fortnightly Review*, XXXVII (June 1885), pp. 862-868.
    Reprinted: *CP*, I, 277-285.

"The Text of Bracton", *Law Quarterly Review*, I (1885), pp. 189-200.
    Reprinted: *CP*, I, 77-90.

1886

«Исследования по социальной истории Англии в средние века» [Investigations into the Social History of Mediaeval England], *ЖМНПр*, № 5 (May 1886), pp. 1-72; № 8 (August 1886), pp. 276-

310; № 9 (September 1886), pp. 58-97; № 11 (November 1886), pp. 1-204; № 12 (December 1886), pp. 285-306.
Dissertation for which the degree of doctor was conferred.

"Molmen and Molland", *English Historical Review*, I (1886), pp. 734-737.

1887

«Исследования по социальной истории Англии в средние века» [Investigations into the Social History of Mediaeval England], *ЖМНПр*, № 4 (April 1886), pp. 189-221; № 5 (May 1887), pp. 18-57.
Continuation and completion of work whose publication commenced in 1886.

Исследования по социальной истории Англии в средние века [Studies on the Social History of England in the Middle Ages]. Спб., тип. В. С. Балашева, 1887. 6, 259 стр. [DLC, LSE, РНБ]
Dissertation for which the degree of doctor was conferred.

«Новости французской исторической литературы» [News of French Historical Literature], *Русская мысль* [Russian Thought] (1887), № 9, (1887), pp. 166-178 (sgd. П.Г.).
Review of: A. Sorel, *L'Europe et la Révolution Française, tome ii. La Chute de la Royauté* (Paris, 1887) and Jean Reville, *La Religion a Rome sous les Severes* (Paris, 1886).

Review of: M. M. Kovalevsky, *Modern Custom and Ancient Law* in: *Русские ведомости* [Russian Gazette], no. 75 (1887).

1888

«Ранке и его школа» [Ranke and His School], *Русская мысль* [Russian Thought], IV(2) (1888), pp. 213-224.

"Bracton's Note Book", *Law Quarterly Review*, IV (1888), pp. 436-441.

Государственное право Англии. Лекции экстраординарного профессора П. Г. Виноградова [State Law of England. Lectures of Professor Extraordinarius P. G. Vinogradoff]. M., 1888.

1889

История Греции [History of Greece]. M., лит. Теофилова, 1889. 364, 144 p.

Review of: Sir Henry Maine, *Étude sur l'histoire du droit*. Paris. E. Thorin, 1889. lxxxvii, 704 p., in: *Law Quarterly Review*, V (1889), p. 79.

Review of: *Pipe Roll of 12 Henry II*, in *Law Quarterly Review*, V (1889), pp. 79-82.

1890

Лекции по истории средних веков, читанные экстраординарным профессором Виноградовым в весеннем семестре 1886/7 [Lectures on the History of the Middle Ages Delivered by Professor Extraordinarius Vinogradov in the Spring Semester 1886/7]. M., Шмелева, 1890. 467, 16 p. [МПГУ]

«Фустель-де-Куланж. Итоги и приемы его ученой работы» [Fustel de Coulanges. His Conclusions and Method], *Русская мысль* [Russian Thought], № 1 (January 1890), pp. 83-104.

«Американская демократия» [American Democracy], *Русская мысль* [Russian Thought], № 11 (November 1890), pp. 62-82; № 12 (December 1890), pp. 53-79.
Review of: James Bryce, *The American Commonwealth* (London, 1888),

published in Russian as Дж. Брайс, Американская республика, transl. В. Н. Неведомский (М., 1889-90). 3 vols.

1891

(ed.), Основы государственного права Англии [Foundations of the State Law of England], transl. O. V. Poltoratskaia. Ed. P. G. Vinogradoff (Спб., 1891). 123 p.
  Edited translation of A. V. Dicey, *The Law of the Constitution of England* (Spb., 1891).

1892

История средних веков. Лекции, читанные орд. проф. Московского университета П. Г. Виноградова [History of the Middle Ages. Lectures Read by Professor Ordinarius of Moscow University, P. G. Vinogradoff] М., лит. Александровской, 1892. 270 стр. [РНБ]
  Lithographed typewritten text.

«И. В. Киреевский и начало Московского славянофильства» [I. V. Kireevskii and the Beginning of the Slavophile Movement in Moscow], *Вопросы философии и психологии* [Questions of Philosophy and Psychology] II, кн. 11 (1892), pp. 98-126.
  Reprinted: *RR*, pp. 47-68.

«Первые главы Афинской политики Аристотеля» [First Chapters of the Athenian Policy of Aristotle], *Филологическое обозрение* [Philological Survey], III, кн. 2 (1892), pp. 97-109.

«Развитие демократии в трактате Аристотеля о государстве афинском» [The Development of Democracy in Aristotle's Constitution of Athens], *Историческое обозрение* [Historical Survey], no. 5 (1892), pp. 156-174.

«Трактат Аристотеля о государстве афинском» [Aristotle's Treatise on the Constitution of Athens], *Русская мысль* [Russian Thought], № 11 (1892), pp. 198-220.

Учебник древней истории [Textbook of Ancient History]. М., т-во Печ. С. П. Яковлева, 1892. 91 стр. [DLC, РНБ]
   Only volume 1 published.

Villainage in England. Oxford, Clarendon Press, 1892. xii, 464 p. [DLC, MH-L]
   Rev.: *English Historical Review*, VII (1892), 444-465 (H. Seebohm); *Political Science Review*, VIII (1893), 653-676 (I. S. Leadam); "perhaps the most important book written on the peasantry of the feudal age and the village community in England; it can only be compared for value with F. W. Maitland's Domesday Book and Beyond", *Encyclopedia Britannica*, XXVIII (11th ed., 1913), p. 100 (anon.).
   Reprinted: London, Oxford University Press, 1927. xii, 464 p. [IHR]
   Reprinted: New York, Russell & Russell, [1967]. [DLC]
   Reprinted: Oxford, Clarendon Press, 1968. [DLC]
   Reprinted: Grosse Pointe, Michigan, Scholarly Press, 1968. [DLC]
   Reprinted: Clark, New Jersey, Lawbook Exchange, 2005. [DLC]

«Влияние рек на происхождение цивилизации» [The Influence of Rivers upon Civilization], *Северный вестник* [Northern Herald], кн. 6, отд. 1 (1892), стр. 33-44.

1893

"Folkland", *English Historical Review*, VIII (1893), pp. 1-17. [MH-L]
   Reprinted: *CP*, I, 91-111.

«Т. Н. Грановский» [T. N. Granovskii], in *Русская энциклопедия* [Russian Encyclopedia], XVIII (1893), pp. 561-563.

«Т. Н. Грановский» [T. N. Granovskii], *Русская мысль* [Russian

Thought], no. 4 (1893), pp. 44-66.
Reprinted: RR, pp. 69-94.

История Греции: Курс лекций, читанных на историко-филологическом факультете Императорского Московского университета 1892-93 г. [History of Greece: Cours of Lectures Read at the Faculty of History and Philology of the Imperial Moscow University 1892-93]. М., б.г. [1893]. 480 стр. [МПГУ]

«Новые работы по истории Греции» [New Works on the History of Greece], *Русская мысль* [Russian Thought], № 3 (1893), pp. 47-54.
Reviews of: E. Abbott, *A History of Greece*. Parts I & II. (London, 1890-92) and of A. von Holm, *Griechische Geschichte*. Parts I-III (Berlin, 1886, 1889, 1891).

«Религиозно-общественный идеал западного христианства в V веке» [Religious-Social Ideal of Western Christianity in the Fifth Century], *Русская мысль* [Russian Thought] no. 7 (1893), pp. 51-58.
Review: Prince E. Trubetskoi (1863-1920), *Религиозно-общественный идеал западного христианства в V веке*. М., тип. Е. Лисснера и Ю. Романа, 1892. ч. 1.

(comp.), *Учебник всеобщей истории: Часть I. Древний мир* [Textbook of Universal History: Ancient World]. М., Книжный магазин И. Дейбнера, 1893. 196 стр. [PSU, РНБ]

Review of: Charles McLean Andrews (1863-1943), *The Old English Manor: A Study in English Economic History* (Baltimore, Johns Hopkins Press, 1892); in *English Historical Review*, VIII (1893), pp. 540-543.

1894

«Кальвин и Женева» [Calvin and Geneva], *Русская мысль* [Russian Thought], № 9 (1894), pp. 134-141.

Review: R. U. Vipper, Церковь и государство в Женеве века в эпоху кальвинизма [Church and State in Geneva in the Sixteenth Century] (M., 1894).

Учебник всеобщей истории: Часть I. Древний мир [Textbook of Universal History: Ancient World]. 2d ed.; М., Книжный маназин И. Дейбнера, 1894. 196 стр. [РНБ]

(comp.), *Учебник всеобщей истории: Часть II. Средние века* [Textbook of Universal History: Medieval World]. М., Книжный магазин И. Дейбнера, 1894. 245 стр. [PSU, РНБ]

«Т. Н. Грановский», in *В пользу воскресных школ: Сборник* [For the Benefit of Sunday Schools: Collection]. М., Издание редакции «Русская мысль», 1894, pp. 65-98. [НБУк]
    Co-edited with A. Azherov, Kh. D. Alchevskaia, K. D. Balmont, and I. I. Ivanov.

1895

Франция перед революцией [France Before the Revolution], Русская мысль [Russian Thought], № 11 (1895), pp. 83-93.
    Review of: M. M. Kovalevskii, Происхождение современной демократии [Origin of Modern Democracy] (М., 1895), vol. 1.

История Греции. Лекции, 1894-1895 [History of Greece. Lectures, 1894-1895]. М., лит. Общества распростренния пол. Книг, 1895. 432 p.

1896

«Альфред Великий» [Alfred the Great], *История средних веков* [History of the Middle Ages], ed. P. G. Vinogradoff. М., 1896, II, pp. 16-30.

«Империя VI века и Юстиниан» [Empire of the VI Century and Justinian], *Книга для чтения по истории средних веков, составленная кружком преподавателей* [Book for Reading on History of Middle Ages Compiled by Circle of Teachers], ed. P. G. Vinogradoff. M., 1896, I, pp. 212-246. [МПГУ]

Книга для чтения по истории средних веков, составленная кружком преподавателей [Book for Reading on History of Middle Ages Compiled by Circle of Teachers], ed. P. G. Vinogradoff. M., 1896, I. 446 p. [МАГУ]
This four-volume series published between 1896-99 was awarded the Peter the Great Prize.

Tocqueville, A. de (1805-1859). *L'Ancien Régime et la Révolution*, ed., transl. and preface of P. G. Vinogradoff. M., тип. А. Г. Кольчугина, 1896. 350 стр. [РНБ]

(comp.), *Учебник всеобщей истории: Часть III. Новое время* [Textbook of Universal History: Modern Times]. 2d corrected ed.; M., Книжный магазин И. Дейбнера, 1896. [4], 248 стр. [PSU, РНБ]

1897

«Альфред Великий» [Alfred the Great], *Книга для чтения по истории средних веков, составленная кружком преподавателей* [Book for Reading on History of Middle Ages Compiled by Circle of Teachers], ed. P. G. Vinogradoff. M., 1897, II(1), pp. 16-30.

История Греции: Лекции, читанные профессором П. Г. Виноградовом на I и III семестрах истор. филол. факультетов 1896-97 ак. г. [History of Greece: Lectures Read by Professor P. G. Vinogradoff at the I and III Semesters of the Faculties of History and Philology, 1896-97 Academic Year]. M., лит. Общества пол. книг, [1897]. 464 стр. [РНБ]

Lithographed typewritten manuscript.
Книга для чтения по истории средних веков, составленная кружком преподавателей [Book for Reading on History of Middle Ages Compiled by Circle of Teachers], ed. P. G. Vinogradoff. M., 1897, 2(1). 456 p. [МАГУ]

«Подготовка феодализма» [Preparation of Feudalism], *Книга для чтения по истории средних веков, составленная кружком преподавателей* [Book for Reading on History of Middle Ages Compiled by Circle of Teachers], ed. P. G. Vinogradoff. M., 1897, II(1), pp. 1-15.

1898

О прогрессе [On Progress]. M., Типо-лит. И. Н. Кушренев, 1898. 62 p. [DLC, MH, РНБ]
   Three lectures delivered in Moscow at the auditorium of the Historical Museum on 4, 5, and 6 February 1898. Other lectures delivered by A. L. Plesterer and S. M. Luk'ianov.

Tocqueville, A. de (1805-1859). *L'Ancien Régime et la Révolution*, ed., transl. and preface of P. G. Vinogradoff. 2d ed.; M., тип. А. Г. Кольчугина, 1898. 350 стр. [РНБ]

1899

«Альфред Великий» [Alfred the Great], *Книга для чтения по истории средних веков, составленная кружком преподавателей* [Book for Reading on History of Middle Ages Compiled by Circle of Teachers], ed. P. G. Vinogradoff. 2d ed.; M., 1899, II(1), pp. 16-30.

"Geschlecht und Verwandtschaft im Altnorwegischen Rechte", *Zeitschrift für Social- und Wirtschaftsgeschichte*, VII(I) (1899), pp. 1-43. [MH-L]

Reprinted: *CP*, II, 46-83.

История Греции: Лекции ординарного профессора П. Г. Виноградова. 1898-99 ак. г. [History of Greece: Lectures of Professor Ordinarius P. G. Vinogradoff. 1898-99 Academic Year]. М., лит. Общества распр. пол. книг, [1899]. 226 стр. [МПГУ, РНБ]

Книга для чтения по истории средних веков, составленная кружком преподавателей [Book for Reading on History of Middle Ages Compiled by Circle of Teachers], ed. P. G. Vinogradoff. 2d ed.; M., 1899, 2. 969 p. [МАГУ]

«Подготовка феодализма» [Preparation of Feudalism], *Книга для чтения по истории средних веков, составленная кружком преподавателей* [Book for Reading on History of Middle Ages Compiled by Circle of Teachers], ed. P. G. Vinogradoff. 2d ed.; M., 1899, II(1), pp. 1-15.

1900

"Agricultural Services", *Economic Journal*, x (1900), 308-322.
Reprinted: *CP*, I, 112-128.

История средних веков. Лекции орд. проф. П. Г. Виноградова, читанные на филологическом факультете Моск. Унив. в 1898 уч. г. [History of Middle Ages. Lectures of Professor Ordinarius P. G. Vinogradoff Read at the Faculty of Philology of Moscow University in the 1898 Academic Year]. 2d ed.; Спб., лит. Богданов, 1899-1900. 303 стр. [РНБ]
Lithographed typewritten text. Addition: Development of State Power in England (1900). 178 p.

Лекции по истории средних веков. Курс 1899-1900 г. [Lectures on History of Middle Ages. Cours for 1899-1900]. М., Б. г., [1900]. 272, vii стр. [МПГУ]

Учебник всеобщей истории: Часть III. Новое время. [Textbook of World History. Part III. Modern Period]. 5th ed.; M., 1900. 246 стр. [МПГУ]

Review of: T. W. Page, *The End of Villainage in England*, in: *English Historical Review* (October 1900), pp. 774-781.
Reprinted: *CP*, I, 129-138.

1901

«Империя VI века и Юстиниан» [Empire of VI Century and Justinian], *Книга для чтения по истории средних веков, составленная кружком преподавателей* [Book for Reading on History of Middle Ages Compiled by Circle of Teachers], ed. P. G. Vinogradoff. 3d ed.; М., 1901, I, pp. 213-247. [МПГУ]

История Греции: Лекции профессора Императорского Московского университета П. Г. Виноградова. 1900/1 г. [History of Greece: Lectures of Professor P. G. Vinogradoff of Imperial Moscow University. 1900/01 Academic Year]. М., тип. Рихтера, [1901]. 398 стр. [МПГУ, РНБ]
    Lithographed typewritten manuscript.

История средних веков. Лекция проф. П. Г. Виноградова. Курс 1901-1902 г.г. [History of Middle Ages. Lectures of Professor P. G. Vinogradoff. Cours for 1901-02] М., типо.-лит. Рихтер, 1901. 167 стр. [РНБ]
    Lithographed typewritten text. Date on cover is 1903.

Книга для чтения по истории средних веков, составленная кружком преподавателей [Book for Reading on History of Middle Ages Compiled by Circle of Teachers], ed. P. G. Vinogradoff. 3d ed.; М., 1901, I. 446 p. [МАГУ, РНБ]

«Учебное дело в наших университетах» [Instruction in Our Universities], *Вестник Европы* [Herald of Europe], no. 10 (1901), pp. 535-573.
    Reprinted: *RR*, pp. 107-140.

1902

«Борьба за школу на Скандинавском севере» [Struggle for School in Scandinavian North], *Вестник Европы* [Herald of Europe], no. 3 (1902), pp. 95-129.

Борьба за школу на скандинавском севере. Публичная лекция, чит. в Москве, 2-го ноября 1902 г. В пользу «Московского Педагогического Общества». [Struggle for School in the Scandinavian North. Public Lecture Read at Moscow, 2 November 1902. For the Benefit of the "Moscow Pedagogical Society"]. Спб., тип. Стасюлевича, 1902. 38, vi стр. [РНБ]

Книга для чтения по истории средних веков, составленная кружком преподавателей [Book for Reading on the History of the Middle Ages Compiled by Circle of Teachers], ed. P. G. Vinogradoff. 2d ed.; М., 1902, 3. 583 p. [МАГУ]

«Комическая фигура» [Comical Figure],, *Освобождение* [Liberation], № 7(31) (1902), pp. 113-115.
    Reprinted: *RR*, pp. 161-166.

"The Meaning of the Present Development in Russia", in F. A. Kirkpatrick (ed), *Lectures on the History of the Nineteenth Century, Delivered at the Cambridge University Extension Summer Meeting August 1902.* Cambridge, University Press, 1902, pp. 257-276.
    Transl.: *RR*, pp. 201-217.

Накануне нового столетия [On the Eve of a New Century]. М., т-во И. Д. Сытина, 1902. 28 стр. (Педагогическое общество, состоящее при Московском университете. Труды Комиссии по устройству чтении для учащихся). [РНБ]

«Новые временные правила» [New Provisional Rules], *Освобождение* [Liberation], № 8 (1902), стр. 116-119.
    Reprinted: *RR*, pp. 154-160.

"The Reforming Work of Tsar Alexander II", in F. A. Kirkpatrick (ed), *Lectures on the History of the Nineteenth Century, Delivered at the Cambridge University Extension Summer Meeting August 1902*. Cambridge, University Press, 1902, pp. 237-256.
    Transl.: *RR*, pp. 185-200.

"Wergeld und Stand", *Zeitschrift der Savignystiftung für Rechtsgeschichte*, XXIII (1902), pp. 123-192. [MH-L]
    Reprinted: *CP*, II, 84-152.

«Задачи правоведения» [The Tasks of Jurisprudence], in *Вступительные лекции профессоров Московского императорского университета: П. Г. Виноградова, А. А, Кизевеннера, А. А. Мануилова, С. А. Муромцева* [Inaugural Lectures of Professors of Moscow Imperial University: P. G. Vinogradoff, A. A. Kizevetter, A. A. Manuilov, S. A. Muromtsev]. [M.], Костромское землячество при Московском университете, [1909]. 99 стр. [DLC, РНБ]

«Что делается и что делать в русских университетах» [What is Being Done and What is to be Done in Russian Universities], *Освобождение* [Liberation], № 2 (1902), стр. 21-23; № 3, стр. 39-40. [pseud.: абв]
    Reprinted: *RR*, pp. 141-153.

Review of: D. M. Petrushevskii, *Восстание Уота Тайлера* [Uprising of Wot Tayler] Спб.-М., 1897-1901. 2 т., in *ЖМНПр*, CCCXXX (1902), pp. 440-449.

Review of: D. M. Petrushevskii, *Восстание Уота Тайлера* [Uprising of Wot Tayler]. Спб.-М., 1897-1901. 2 т., in: *Deutsche Literaturzeitung*, XXIII (22 February 1902), pp. 487-491.

Review of: Henri Eugène Sée (1864-1936), *Classes rurales et le régime domanial en France au Moyen Age* (Paris, Giard & Briere, 1901), in: *English Historical Review*, XVII (1902), 328-332.

1903

«Альфред Великий» [Alfred the Great], *Книга для чтения по истории средних веков, составленная кружком преподавателей* [Book for Reading on History of Middle Ages Compiled by Circle of Teachers], ed. P. G. Vinogradoff. 3d ed.; М., 1903, II(1), pp. 16-30.

Книга для чтения по истории средних веков, составленная кружком преподавателей [Book for Reading on History of Middle Ages Compiled by Circle of Teachers], ed. P. G. Vinogradoff. 3d ed.; М., 1903, 2(1). 445 p. [МАГУ]

Книга для чтения по истории средних веков, составленная кружком преподавателей [Book for Reading on History of Middle Ages Compiled by Circle of Teachers], ed. P. G. Vinogradoff. 3d ed.; М., 1903, 2(2). 527 p. [МАГУ]

Книга для чтения по истории средних веков, составленная кружком преподавателей [Book for Reading on History of Middle Ages Compiled by Circle of Teachers], ed. P. G. Vinogradoff. 2d ed.; М., 1903, 4. 496 p. [МАГУ]

Местное самоуправление в Англии [Local Government in England]. Сиб., тип. т-ва «Общественная польза», [1903]. 33 стр. [РНБ]

«Местное самоуправление в Англии» [Local Government in England], in *Мелкая земская единица* [Little Zemstvo Entity]. (Спб., [1903]), стр. 62-93.

«Подготовка феодализма» [Preparation of Feudalism], *Книга для чтения по истории средних веков, составленная кружком преподавателей* [Book for Reading on History of Middle Ages Compiled by Circle of Teachers], ed. P. G. Vinogradoff. 3d ed.; М., 1897, II(1), pp. 1-15.

The Reforming Work of the Tzar Alexander II. And The Meaning of the Present Development in Russia. [Cambridge, England, Cambridge

University Press, 1903]. 40 p.
Reprinted from *Lectures on History in the 19th Century Given at the Summer Meeting 1902.*

Средние века. Лекции профессора П. Г. Виноградова [the Middle Ages. Lectures of Professor P. G. Vinogradoff]. М., типо.-лит. В. Рихтер, 1903. 351 стр. [МПГУ, РНБ]
Lithographed typewritten manuscript.

Учебник всеобщей истории: Новое время [Textbook of World History. Modern Period]. 7th ed.; М., 1903. ч. 3. 245 стр. [МПГУ]

1904

«Аграрный кризис в Римской империи» [The Agrarian Crisis in the Roman Empire], *Научное слово* [Scientific Word], № 4 (1904), pp. 56-69. [МПГУ]

«О некоторых особенностях родового строя уэльских кельтов» [On Certain Peculiarities of the Kinship Structure of Welsh Celts], *Сборник статей по истории права, посвященный М. Ф. Владимирскому-Буданову* [Collected Articles on the History of Law Dedicated to M. F. Vladimirskii-Budanov]. Киев, 1904, стр. 141-152.

"The Peasant Caste in Russia", *Independent Review*, IV, no 13 (1904), pp. 89-101.
Transl.: *RR*, pp. 218-228.

'Sulung and Hide", *English Historical Review*, XIX (1904), 282-286.

"The Teaching of Sir Henry Maine", *Law Quarterly Review*, XX (1904), 119-133.

"The Teaching of Sir Henry Maine", *Revue de Sociologie*, XII (1904), pp. 797-813.

The Teaching of Sir Henry Maine: An Inaugural Lecture Delivered in Corpus Christi College Hall on March 1, 1904. London, H. Frowde, 1904. 19 p. [MH-L]
    Rev.: *English Historical Review*, XIX (1904), 825-826 [D.]

«Учение сэра Генри Мэна» [The Teaching of Sir Henry Maine], *Научное слово* [Scientific Word], VIII (1904), pp. 59-75.

Review of: Alexander Savin (1873-1923), *Английская деревня в эпоху Тюдоров* [English Village in the Tudor Era]. xiii, 485 p., in *ЖМНПр*, CCCLV (1904), pp. 222-232.

1905

«Государственный строй Англии» [State Structure of England], in *Политический строй современных государств: сборник статей* [Political System of Contemporary States: Collection of Articles]. Спб., Тип. Сиб. акц. общ. печ. и пищебум. дела в России «Слово», 1905-06. 2 т. [MH-L]
    Publication of Prince P. D. Dolgorukii and I. I. Petrunkevich with the participation of the editorial board of the newspaper "Pravda". Vinogradoff's piece appears in volume 1, pp. 191-271.

The Growth of the Manor. London/New York, Swan Sonnenschein & Co./The Macmillan Co., 1905. vii, 384 p. [DLC, IHR, MH-L]
    Rev.: *American Historical Review*, XI (1906), 361-365; *English Historical Review*, XXI (1906), 764-767 (F. G. M. Beck); *Law Quarterly Review*, XXI (1905), 294-300 (William Paley Baildon); *Revue hist.*, CXV (1907), 126-128; *The Speaker* (May 1905) (E. Jenks); *Times Literary Supplement* (1905), 322.

«Политические письма» [Political Letters], *Русские ведомости* [Russian Gazette], no. 210 (5 August 1905), no. 219 (14 August 1905), no. 224 (19 August 1905).
Reprinted: *RR*, pp. 237-254.

«Предметные уроки» [Subject Lessons], *RR*, pp. 265-270.
First published from Harvard Law School Archive; undated and possibly prepared for publication in *Голос Москвы*.

«17-го октября 1905 года» [17 October 1905], *Слово* [Word], no. 300 (14 November 1905), no. 301 (15(28) November 1905).
Reprinted: *RR*, pp. 255-264.

"Zur Wergeldfrage", *Vierteljahrsschrift für Social- und Wirtschaftsgeschichte*, IV (1905), 534-553. [MH-L]
Addresses Heck's theory.
Reprinted: *CP*, II, 153-172.

Transl.: *История века (Западная Европа и внеевропейские государства)* [History of the Age (Western Europe and Non-European States)], ed. E. Lavisse (1842-1922) and A. Rambeau (1842-1905). Transl. from the French with additional articles by P. G. Vinogradoff, M. M. Kovalevskii, and K. A. Timiriazev. М., т-во «Бр. А. и И. Гранат и К°», 1905. 32 стр.
Chapters 1 and 2 of Volume 2(1).

Ed.: Dicey, Arthur Venn (1835-1922), *Основы государственного права Англии* [Foundations of the State Law of England], ed. P. G. Vinogradoff. Transl. O. V. Poltoratskaia. М., тип. И. Д. Сытина, 1905. xxxvi, 658 p.
Translation of the sixth English edition of *Introduction to the Study of the Law of the Constitution*.

Review of: William Sharp McKechnie, *Magna Carga: A Commentary on the Great Charter of King John, with an Historical Introduction* (Glasgow, 1905). xix, 607 p. in: *Law Quarterly Review*, XXI (1905), 250-257.

Review of: Dm. Petrushevskii, *Восстание Уота Тайлера. Очерки из истории разложения феодального строя в Англии. Часть первая. Спб., 1897.* [Uprising of Wat Tayler. Essays on the History of the Breakdown of the Feudal System in England]. Спб., тип. Имп. Академии наук, 1905. 20 стр. [МПГУ, РНБ]

Pamphlet form published by Russian Academy of Sciences and awarded the Metropolitan Makarii Gold Medal. Offprint from *Отчет о 10 присуждении премии митрополитана Макарии* (1905).

1906

«Возможно ли было образование либерального министерства» [Is the Formation of Liberal Ministry Possible?], *Московский еженедельник* [Moscow Weekly], № 20 (1906), стр. 11-16.

Reprinted: RR, pp. 295-299. The article was written at St. Blasien, 4 August 1906.

"The First Month of the Duma", *Independent Review*, x, no. 34 (1906), pp. 48-63.

Transl.: RR, pp. 281-294.

«Империя VI века и Юстиниан» [Empire of VI Century and Justinian], *Книга для чтения по истории средних веков, составленная кружком преподавателей* [Book for Reading on History of Middle Ages Compiled by Circle of Teachers], ed. P. G. Vinogradoff. 4th ed.; M., 1906, I, pp. 214-248. [МПГУ]

Introduction of a Thesis into the Modern History School. Oxford, B. H. Blackwell, 1906. 11 p. (with Charles Harding Firth (1857-1936)).

История средних веков. Лекция орд. проф. Московского университета П. Г. Виноградова [History of the Middle Ages. Lecture of Professor Ordinarius P. G. Vinogradoff of Moscow University]. 3d ed.; Спб., 1906. 392, 218, 29 стр. [РНБ]

Lithographed typewritten text.

Книга для чтения по истории средних веков, составленная кружком преподавателей [Book for Reading on History of the Middle Ages Compiled by Circle of Teachers], ed. P. G. Vinogradoff. 4th ed.; M., 1906, I. 448 p. [МАГУ]

"Russia at the Parting of the Ways", *Fortnightly Review*, LXXIX (N.S., 1906), pp. 1016-1025.
Transl.: *RR*, pp. 271-280.

Сборник законодательных памятников древнего западно-европейского права [Collection of Legislative Monuments of Medieval Western-European Law], ed. P. G. Vinogradoff and M. F. Vladimirskii-Budanov (1838-1916). Киев, Н. Т. Корчак-Новицкий, 1906-08. 3 т. [DLC, MH-L; МПГУ, РНБ]
Том 1: Lex Salica (ed. with annotations by D. N. Egorov) 326 p.
Том 2: Lex Saxonum (ed. with annotations by V. S. Protopopov). 74 p.
Originally published: *Университетские известия* (1904-06).

Review of: L. M. Larson, *The King's Household in England Before the Norman Conquest* (Bulletin of the University of Wisconsin, No. 100, History Series I, No. 2), pp. 55-204, in *Zeitschrift für Rechtsgeschichte*, XXVII (1906), pp. 373-374.

1907

"An Illustration of the Continuity of the Openfield System", *Quarterly Journal of Economics*, IV (1907), 62-82.
Reprinted: *CP*, I, 139-148.

"By-Laws of an Oxfordshire Manor", *Quarterly Journal of Economics*, IV (1907), pp. 13-21. [MH-L]
Reprinted: *CP*, I, 286-296.

"Frederick William Maitland", *English Historical Review*, XXII (1907), pp. 280-289.
Reprinted: *CP*, I, 253-264.

«Итоги XIX века» [Results of the Nineteenth Century], *История XIX века (Западная Европа и внеевропейские государства)* [History of the XIX Century (Western Europe and Non-European States], ed. E. Lavisse (1842-1922) and A. Rambeau (1842-1905). Transl. from the French with additional articles by P. G. Vinogradoff, M. M. Kovalevskii, and K. A. Timiriazev. M., т-во «Бр. А. и И. Гранат и К°», 1907. 8 т. [LSE, РНБ]
   Vinogradoff's contribution appears in volume 8, pp. 249-269 [LSE].

"Transfer of Land in Old English Law", *Harvard Law Review*, xx (1907), 532-548. [MH]
   Reprinted: *CP*, I, 149-167.

Учебник всеобщей истории: Древней мир [Textbook of World History: Ancient World]. 10th ed.; M., 1907. ч. 1. 186 стр. [МПГУ]

Review of: Alexander Savin (1873-1923), *Английская секуляризация* [English Secularization]. (M., 1906). 576 p. in *ЖМНПр*, xii (1907), pp. 429-432.

Review of Frances Gardiner Davenport (1870-1927), *The Economic Development of a Norfolk Manor, 1086-1565* (Cambridge, Cambridge University Press, 1906), x, 105, cii p., in *English Historical Review*, xxii (1907), pp. 154-156.

1908

"Aristotle on Legal Redress", *Columbia Law Review*, viii (November 1908), pp. 1-13. [MH-L]

[?] "By-Laws of an Oxfordshire Manor", *Quarterly Journal of Economics*, xxii (1908), pp. 13-21. [MH-L]
   Reprinted: *CP*, I, 286-296.

English Society in the Eleventh Century: Essays in English Mediaeval History.
Oxford, Clarendon Press, 1908. xii, 599 p. [DLC, IHR, MH-L]
  Rev.: *American Historical Review,* XIV (1909), 102-104; *English Historical Review,* XXIV (1909), 333-336 (James Tait]); *Revue hist.,* CI (1909), 147-148; *Times Literary Supplement* (1908), p. 171; *ЖМНПр,* xxiv (1909), 169-216, 399-436 (D. M. Petrushevskii; also separate booklet. Спб., Сенатская тип., 88 p.).
  Reprinted: Oxford, Clarendon Press, 1968. [DLC]
  Reprinted: Grosse Pointe, Michigan, Scholarly Press, 1968. [DLC]
  Reprinted: Clark, New Jersey, Lawbook Exchange, 2005. [DLC]

"A History of Local Government", *The Nation,* 2 May 1908, p. 162.
  Review of: Sidney and Beatrice Webb, *English Local Government from the Revolution to the Municipal Corporations Act,* vols. 2 and 3: The Manor and the Borough.
  Reprinted: *CP,* I, 303-307.

"An Illusion of Continuity", *Quarterly Journal of Economics,* XII (1908), 62-73.

История правоведения: (курс для историков и юристов), лекции, читанные в Императорском Московском Университете в осеннем семестре 1908-9 года [History of Jurisprudence: (Cours for Historians and Jurists), Lectures Read at Imperial Moscow University in Autumn Semester of 1908-09]. М., изд. Студентов А. Ф. Изюмова и Н. П. Невзорова, 1908. 224 стр. [DLC, MH-L, РНБ]
  Lithographed typewritten manuscript.

«О значении городского Народного Университета им. А. Л. Шанявского» [On the Significance of the Shaniavskii City People's University], *Русские ведомости* [Russian Gazette], 2 October 1908.

«Партийное законодательство» [Party Legislation], *Слово* [Word], no. 642 (6(19) December 1908).
  Reprinted: *RR,* pp. 300-304.

«Проект нового университетского устава» [Draft of New University Charter], *Русские ведомости* [Russian Gazette], 17 October 1908, p. 1.
Reprinted: *RR*, pp. 167-172.

"Reason and Conscience in Sixteenth-Century Jurisprudence", *Law Quarterly Review*, XXIV (1908), 373-384.
Reprinted: *CP*, II, 190-204.

"Romanistische Einflüsse im Angelsächsischen Recht: Das Buchland", *Mélanges Fitting*, II (1908), pp. 499-522. [MH-L]

«Школа и воспитание» [School and Nurturing], *RR*, pp. 178-184.
Published for the first time from the Vinogradoff Archive at Harvard Law School. Date is approximate.

1909

Аристотель о восстановлении нарушенного права [Aristotle on the Restoration of a Violated Right]. [Спб.], тип. В. Д. Смирнова, [1909]. 13, [3] стр. [РНБ]

«Аристотель о восстановлении нарушенного права» [Aristotle on the Restoration of a Violated Right], *Гермес: научно-популярный вестник античного мира* [Hermes: Scientific-Popular Herald of Ancient World], no. 6 (1909), pp. 252-256; no. 7 (1909).

«Годичная книга английских судов, как исторический источник» [Yearbook of English Courts as an Historical Source], *Сборник статей, посвященных В. О. Ключевскому* его учениками, друзьямим и почитателями ко дню тридцатилетия его профессорской деятельности в Московском Университете (5 декабря -1879 – 5 декабря 1909 года) [Collected Articles Dedicated to V. O. Kliuchevskii by His Pupils, Friends, and Readers on the Thirtieth Jubilee of His Professorial Activity in Moscow University (5 December 1879 to 5

December 1909] (M., Т-во «Печатня С.П. Яковлева, 1909), II, pp. 427-434.

Конспект к курсу «Истории правоведения», читанные в Московском университете в осеннем семестре 1908 г. [Synopsis for Cours "History of Jurisprudence" Read at Moscow University in Autumn Semester of 1908]. М., Изд. Студента А. Ф. Изюмова, 1909. 14 стр. [DLC, MH-L, РНБ]
  Lithographed typewritten manuscript.

Краткий обзор истории Греции и Рима (систематические указатели алфавитный и хронологический) [Concise Survey of History of Greece and Rome (Systematic Indexes, Alphabetical and Chronological]. Киев, тип. Петрушевский, 1909. 222 стр. [РНБ]

"Die Praxis der Englischen Staatseinrichtungen", *Zeitschrift für Politik*, II (1909), pp. 141-158.
  Review of Lawrence Lowell, *The Government of England* (1908); Sidney Low, *The Governance of England* (1904).
  Reprinted: *CP*, I, 308-326.

"Preface", in Alexander Nikolaevich Savin (1873-1923), *English Monasteries on the Eve of Dissolution*. Francis de Zulueta (1878-1958), *Patronage in the Later Empire*. (Oxford, Clarendon Press, 1909), pp. iii-vi (Oxford Studies in Social and Legal History, 1. Ed. Sir Paul Vinogradoff). [MH-L]

Roman Law in Mediaeval Europe. London/New York, Harper & Brothers, 1909. vii, 135 p. [DLC, MH-L]
  Reprinted: Cambridge, England/ New York, Speculum Historiale/ Barnes & Noble, 1968. 155 p.
  Reprinted: Foreword by Peter Stein. Holmes Beach, Florida, William Gaunt, 1994. 155 p. [MH-L]
  Reprinted: Union, New Jersey, Lawbook Exchange, 2001. vii, 135 p. [DLC, MH-L]
  Italian transl.: *Il diritto Romano nella Europa mediovale*, transl. Salvatore Roccobono (1864-1958). Palermo, A. Reber, 1914). xvi, 141 p. [MH-L]

(2d ed.; Preface by Francis de Zulueta (1878-1958). Oxford, Clarendon Press, 1929). 155 p. [MH-L]
Rev.: *Harvard Law Review*, XLIII (1929), 150 (Max Radin).
Italian transl.: *Diritto romano nell'Europa medioevale*, transl. Salvatore Roccobono. Milano, Giuffrè, 1950. 114 p. [MH-L]
(3d ed.; Preface by F. de Zulueta. Oxford, Oxford University Press, 1961). 155 p. [MH] (unchanged reprint of 1929 edition).
Japanese transl.: *Chūsei Yōroppa ni okeru Rōma hō*, transl. Ichio Yata, Kensuke Kobori, and Yoshinori Sanada. Tokyo, Chūō daigaku, [1967]. 6, 198, 6, 8 p. [MH-L]
Turkish transl.: *Ortacag Avrupasinda Roma Hukuku*, transl. Ferhat Duzgoren, Sevtap Metin, Ahmet Ulvi Turkbag, Erol Oz, and Taner Ayanoglu. Istanbul, Gocebe Yayinlari, 1997. 128 p.
Spanish transl.: *Derecho en la Europa medieval: proceso formative, Francia, Inglaterra y Alemania*. Barcelona, Catedra de Histroaia del Derecho y de las Instituciones, Universidad de Málaga, 2000. 178 p.
Also includes H. Bérard, *Derecho romano en Escocia* (Paris, 1926).

«Университетский вопрос» [University Question], *Русские ведомости* [Russian Gazette], 1 January 1909, p. 9.
Reprinted: *RR*, pp. 173-177.

Review of: H. D. Hazeltine (1871-1960), *Die Geschichte des englischen Pfandrechts*, ed. O. Gierke (Breslau, M. & H. Marcus, 1907), in *English Historical Review*, XXIV (1909), 555-566.

1910

«Империя VI века и Юстиниан» [Empire of the VI Century and Justinian], *Книга для чтения по истории средних веков, составленная кружком преподавателей* [Book for Reading on History of Middle Ages Compiled by Circle of Teachers], ed. P. G. Vinogradoff. 5th ed.; M., 1910, I, pp. 214-248. [МПГУ]

Книга для чтения по истории средних веков, составленная кружком преподавателей [Book for Reading on History of Middle Ages

Compiled by Circle of Teachers], ed. P. G. Vinogradoff. 5th ed.; M., 1910, I. 448 p. [МАГУ]

Книга для чтения по истории средних веков, составленная кружком преподавателей [Book for Reading on History of Middle Ages Compiled by Circle of Teachers], ed. P. G. Vinogradoff. 3d ed.; M., 1910, 3. 584 p. [МАГУ]

«Отзыв о сочинении А. Н. Савина а) «Английская деревня в эпоху Тюдоров». Москва, 1903; б) «Английская секуляризация», Москва, 1906» [Review of Work of A. N. Savin (a) English Village During the Tudor Era, Moscow, 1903; (b) English Secularization, Moscow, 1906], *Отчет о тринадцатом присуждении Императорскую Академию наук премии Митрополита Макарии* [Report on Thirteenth Award to Imperial Academy of Sciences of Metropolitan Macarius Prize] Спб., 1910. 9 стр. [LSE]

«Практика английских государственных учреждений» [Practice of English State Institutions], in Sidney Lowe, *Государственный строй Англии.* [State System of England]. С вступительными замечаниями и статей проф. П. Г. Виноградова. М., 1910, стр. 3-50.

"Preface", in Sir Frank Murray Stenton (1880-1967), *Types of Manorial Structure in the Northern Danelaw.* Oxford, Clarendon Press, 1910), pp. iii-iv (Oxford Studies in Social and Legal History, 2. Ed. Sir Paul Vinogradoff).

Римское право в средневековой Европе [Roman Law in Middle Ages Europe]. М., Изд. А. А. Карцева, 1910. 99 стр. [DLC, MH-L, РНБ]
  Based on lectures delivered at the University of London in 1909. First published in English during that year.

«Средневековое поместье в Англии» [Middle Ages Estate in England], *ЖМНПр*, xxx (1910), 290-337 (cont.).

Учебник всеобщей истории: Новое время [Textbook of World History: Modern Period]. 11th ed.; М., 1910. ч. 3. 245 стр. [МПГУ]

1911

"Anglo-Saxon Law", in *Encyclopedia Britannica* (11th ed.; Cambridge, at the University Press, 1910-11), II, pp. 35-38.

"Folkland", in *Encyclopedia Britannica* (11th ed.; Cambridge, at the University Press, 1910-11), X, pp. 600-601.

«Германское право» [German Law], *Энциклопедический словарь Гранат* [Encyloopedic Dictionary of Granat] (М., 1914), XIV, cols. 212-239.

Господство права. Лекция П. Г. Виноградова, Московского и Оксфордского университетов [Rule of Law. Lecture of P. G. Vinogradoff, Moscow and Oxford Universities]. М., тип. т-ва И. Д. Сытина, 1911. 35 стр. (Московское общество народных университетов) [LSE, РНБ]

The Growth of the Manor (2d rev. ed.; London/New York, George Allen & Unwin/The Macmillan Co., 1911). ix, 384 p. [IHR, MH-L]
    Reissued: London, Allen & Unwin, [1951]. [MH-L]
    Reprinted: New York, Augustus M. Kelley, 1968. [MH-L]
    Reprinted: Clark, New Jersey, Lawbook Exchange, 2005.

История XIX века (Западная Европа и внеевропейские государства) [History of the Century (Western Europe and Non-European States], ed. E. Lavisse (1842-1922) and A. Rambeau (1842-1905). Transl. from the French with additional articles by P. G. Vinogradoff,

М. М. Kovalevskii, and К. А. Timiriazev. М., т-во «Бр. А. и И. Гранат и К°», 1911. 324 стр. [РНБ]
Volume one only.

"Jurisprudence, Comparative", in *Encyclopedia Britannica* (11th ed.; Cambridge, at the University Press, 1910-11), XV, pp. 580-587.

"Manor", in *Encyclopedia Britannica* (11th ed.; Cambridge, at the University Press, 1910-11), XVII, pp. 594-596.

"Serfdom", in *Encyclopedia Britannica* (11th ed.; Cambridge, at the University Press, 1910-11), XXIV, pp. 664-666.

"Socage", in *Encyclopedia Britannica* (11th ed.; Cambridge, at the University Press, 1910-11), XXV, p. 300.

Средневековое поместье в Англии [Middle Ages Estate in England]. Спб., Сенатская тип., 1911. 366 стр. [МПГУ, РНБ]

«Средневековое поместье в Англии» [Middle Ages Estate in England], *ЖМНПр*, XXXI (1911), 142-176, 319-368; XXXII (1911), 99-123, 264-326; XXXIII (1911), 70-98, 193-224; XXXIV (1911), 42-60, 177-206; XXXV (1911), 1-39.

"Succession", in *Encyclopedia Britannica* (11th ed.; Cambridge, at the University Press, 1910-11), XXV, pp. 2-5.

"Village Communities", in *Encyclopedia Britannica* (11th ed.; Cambridge, at the University Press, 1910-11), XXVIII, pp. 68-73.

"Villenage", in *Encyclopedia Britannica* (11th ed.; Cambridge, at the University Press, 1910-11), XXVIII, pp. 81-84.

Review of: Karl von Amira (1848-1930), *Der Stab in der germanischen Rechtssymbolik* (Munich, n.p., 1909), in *English Historical Review*, XXVI (1911), pp. 561-562.

Review of: H. A. L. Fisher (ed.), *The Collected Papers of Frederic William Maitland* (Cambridge, Cambridge University Press, 1911). 3 vols., in *The Nation* (15 July 1911), pp. 578-579.

1912

"Ceorl", in J. Hoops (ed.), *Real-leksikon der Germanischen Alterumskunde* (Strasburg, Verlag von Karl J. Trubner, 1912), pp. 368-369.

"Dorfverfassung [C. England]" in J. Hoops (ed.), *Real-leksikon der Germanischen Alterumskunde* (Strasburg, Verlag von Karl J. Trubner, 1912), pp. 483-485.

"Preface", in Eleanor Constance Lodge (1869-1936), *The Estates of the Archbishop and Chapter of Saint André of Bordeaux under English Rule*. Arthur Wilfred Ashby (1886-1953), *One Hundred years of Poor Law Administration in a Warwickshire Village*. Oxford, Clarendon Press, 1912), pp. iii-v (Oxford Studies in Social and Legal History, 3. Ed. Sir Paul Vinogradoff).
Reprinted: New York, Octagon Books, 1974.

[Obituary: Seebohm], *The Times*, 7 February 1912, p. 11.

"Obituary.—Frederic Seebohm (1833-1912)", *Economic Journal* (1912), pp. 338-342.
Reprinted: *CP*, I, 272-276.

«Сибом (Сибом Ф., английский историк)» [Seebohm (F. Seebohm, English Historian], *Русская мысль* [Russian Thought], № 8 (1912), pp. 41-45.

1913

Common Sense in Law. London, Thornton Butterworth, 1913. 256 p. (Home University Library of Modern Knowledge, 80)
Rev.: *Law Quarterly Review*, XXX (1914), 236: "We know very few short books, and not many books on a larger scale, so well fitted to give lay people a just notion of the spirit of modern law, and what is not less important, to encourage practicing lawyers in maintaining a liberal and dignified view of their profession" (Frederick Pollock).
First printing was December 1913. Reprinted ten times by 1933 in this version.
London, Williams and Norgate, 1913. 256 p.
London/New York, Williams & Norgate/Henry Holt, [1914]. 256 p. [DLC, M-L] (Home University Library of Modern Knowledge, 80).
Reprinted: London, Oxford University Press, 1914.
Reprinted: London, Williams and Norgate, 1920. v, 256 p.
Reprinted: London,Williams and Norgate, 1923. 256 p.
Reprinted: London, Thornton Butterworth, 1933. 252 p. (Home University Library of Modern Knowledge, 83) [MH-L]
Reprinted: London, Oxford University Press, 1943. v, 256 p. (with revisions)
(2d. ed.; Edited by Harold Greville Hanbury (b. 1898). London/New York, Oxford University Press, 1946). 192 p. (Home University Library of Modern Knowledge, 83) [DLS, MH-L].
Reprinted: London, Oxford University Press, 1949. 192 p.
Reprinted: London, Oxford University Press, 1956. 192 p.
([3d ed.]; Edited by Harold Greville Hanbury. London/New York, Oxford University Press, [1959]. 192 p. (Home University Library of Modern Knowledge, 83). [MH-L]
Reprinted: New York, Arno Press, 1975. [DCL]
Reprinted: Westport, Connecticut, Greenwood Press, 1987. [DCL]
Reprinted: Clark, New Jersey, Lawbook Exchange, 2006. [DCL]
Translation: *Introducción al derecho*, transl. Vicente Herrero. Mexico, Fondo de Cultura Económica, 1952. 187 p. (Breviarios del Fondo de Cultura Económica, 57). [MH-L]; reprinted, 1957 [MH-L]
Translation: *Il Sense commune nel diritto*, transl. S. Rodatà. Milano, Giuffrè, 1965. 12, 172 p.
Translation: *Hō ni okeru jōshiki*, ed. Suenobu Sanji (1899-1989) and

Ito Masami (b. 1919). Tokyo, Iwanami Shoten, 1972. 261, 11 p. [MH-L]; Reprinted, 2004. [MH-L]

"Constitutional History and the Year Books", *Law Quarterly Review*, XXIX (1913), 272-284. [MH-L]
   Contains the Creighton Lecture, delivered at the invitation of the University of London, 3 February 1913.
   Reprinted: *CP*, I, 192-206.

Constitutional History and the Year Books. [London, 1913]. 12 p. [MH-L]
   Offprint of the above article.

(ed.). *Essays in Legal History Read Before the International Congress of Historical Studies Held in London in 1913*. London, Oxford University Press, 1913. viii, 396 p. [DLC, IHR, MH-L]
   Reprinted: Nendeln, Liechtenstein, Kraus Reprint, 1972. viii, 396 p. [IHR]
   Reprinted: Holmes Beach, Florida, Gaunt, 1993. [MH-L]
   Reprinted: Clark, New Jersey, Lawbook Exchange, 2004. [DLC]

"Geistlichkeit" [B. England]", in J. Hoops (ed.), *Realleksikon der Germanischen Alterumskunde* (Strasburg, Verlag von Karl J. Trubner, 1913), p. 144.

"Halbfreie", in J. Hoops (ed.), *Realleksikon der Germanischen Alterumskunde* (Strasburg, Verlag von Karl J. Trubner, 1913), pp. 364-365.

«Империя VI века и Юстиниан» [Empire of VI Century and Justinian], *Книга для чтения по истории средних веков, составленная кружком преподавателей* [Book for Reading on History of Middle Ages Compiled by Circle of Teachers], ed. P. G. Vinogradoff. 6th ed.; M., 1913, I, pp. 214-248. [МПГУ]

Книга для чтения по истории средних веков, составленная кружком преподавателей [Book for Reading on History of Middle Ages Compiled by Circle of Teachers], ed. P. G. Vinogradoff. 6th ed.; M., 1913, I. 448 p. [МАГУ]

"Presidential Address", in P. G. Vinogradoff (ed.). *Essays in Legal History Read Before the International Congress of Historical Studies Held in London in 1913*. London, Oxford University Press, 1913, pp. 3-12.

Review of: Ludwig Mitteis (1859-1921) and U. Wilcken, *Grundzüge und Chrestomathie der Papyrus-kunde*, in: *Klio: Beiträge zu alten Geschichte*, XIII (1913). (with Harold Idris Bell (1879-19?).

1914

"Grundherrschaft [B. England]", in J. Hoops (ed.), *Real-leksikon der Germanischen Alterumskunde* (Strasburg, Verlag von Karl J. Trubner, 1914), pp. 333-335.

"A Note on the Ancient Demesne", *Law Quarterly Review*, XXX (1914), 499-501.

"Preface", in Willard Titus Barbour (18?-1920), *The History of Contract in Early English Equity*. George William Coopland (1875-1975), *The Abbey of St. Bertin and its Neighbourhood, 900-1350*. Oxford, Clarendon Press, 1914), pp. iii-vii (Oxford Studies in Social and Legal History, 4. Ed. Sir Paul Vinogradoff).
Reprinted: New York, Octagon Books, 1974. 166 p.

Records of the Social and Economic History of England and Wales, ed. P. G. Vinogradoff, Thomas Frederick Tout, et al. London, The British Academy, 1914-1935. 8 vols.
Vinogradoff co-edited volume 1 of the series only.

"Russia: The Psychology of a Nation", *The Times*, 14 September 1914.
Also appeared in pamphlet form, translated into many languages.
Transl.: RR, pp. 305-312.

Russia, the Psychology of a Nation. London/New York, Oxford University Press, H. Milford, [1914]. 13 p. (Oxford Pamphlets, 1914 [no. 12]. [DLC, MH]
Dutch transl.: *Rusland: de ziel van een natie.* London/ Edinburgh, Thomas Nelson & Sons, 1914. 11 p.
French transl.: *La Russie: psychologie d'une nation.* London, Eyres & Spottiswoode, [1914]. 9 p.
Italian transl.: *La Russia: la psicologia di una nazione* [London, Harrison and Sons, 1914]. 7 p.
Swedish transl.: *Ryssland: ett folks psykologi.* London, Thomas Nelson, [1914]. 8 p.
Transl.: *A Russia: psychologia de uma naçao.* London, Eyre & Spottiswoode, [1914]. 8 p.
Transl.: *Rusland: et lands psychologi.* London, Harrison and Sons, 1915. 8 p.

"The Russian Problem", *Yale Review*, XIV (n.s., 1914), pp. 267-282.
Transl.: RR, pp. 313-325.

The Russia Problem. London, Constable and Company Ltd., [1914]. viii, 44 p. [DLC, MH-L]
Contains two essays: "Russia After the War" and "The Psychology of a Nation".

The Russian Problem. New York, George H. Doran Co., [c. 1914]. viii, 44 p. [DLC, MH]
Text of lecture delivered at Sheffield and Nottingham and first published as article in *Russia After the War* (London).

Survey of the Honour of Denbigh 1334, ed. P. Vinogradoff and Frank Morgan (1860-19?). London, Published for The British Academy by H. Milford, 1914. 347 p. [DLC, IHR, MH-L]

Учебник всеобщей истории: Древний мир [Textbook of World History. Ancient World]. 12th ed.; М., Издание А. А. Карцева, 1914. ч. 1. viii, 191 стр.

"United Russia", *Saturday Review*, 19 September 1914.

"Zur Geschichte der englischer Klassifikation der Vermögensarten" in *Heinrich Brunner zum 70. Geburstag von Schülen und Verehrem dargebrachten Festschrift* (Weimar, Hermann Böhlaus, [1914]), pp. 573-577.

Review of: Alfons Dopsch (1868-1953), *Die Wirtschaftsentwicklung der Karolingerzeit: vornehmlich in Deutschland* (Cologne, Hermann Böhlau, 1912-13). 2 vols. in: *English Historical Review*, XXIX (1914), 133-141.

1915

«Альфред Великий» [Alfred the Great], *Книга для чтения по истории средних веков, составленная кружком преподавателей* [Book for Reading on History of Middle Ages Compiled by Circle of Teachers], ed. P. G. Vinogradoff. 5th ed.; М., 1915, II(1), pp. 18-32.

«Английское общественное мнение и война» [English Public Opinion and The War], *Биржевые ведомости* [Stock Exchange Gazette], no. 14696 (27 February/12 March 1915).
Reprinted: *RR*, pp. 332-341.

«Англия и Россия» [England and Russia], *Биржевые ведомости* [Stock-Exchange Gazette], no. 14612 (15/28 January 1915).
Reprinted: *RR*, pp. 326-331.

"The Causes of the War", *Scientia*, XVII (Bologna, 1915), pp. 426-436.
Transl.: *RR*, pp. 342-351.

"Growth of Provincial Self-Government", *The Times Russian Supplement*, 26 April 1915.
Transl.: RR, pp. 229-235.

Книга для чтения по истории средних веков, составленная кружком преподавателей [Book for Reading on History of Middle Ages Compiled by Circle of Teachers], ed. P. G. Vinogradoff. M., 1915, 2. 971 p. [МАГУ]

Очерки по теории права [Essays on the Theory of Law]. М., Т-во Скоропечатни А. А. Левенсон, 1915. 153 p. [DLC, MH-L, РНБ]
Published first in England and the United States simultaneously as *Common-Sense in Law* (1913).

«Подготовка феодализма» [Preparation of Feudalism], *Книга для чтения по истории средних веков, составленная кружком преподавателей* [Book for Reading on History of Middle Ages Compiled by Circle of Teachers], ed. P. G. Vinogradoff. 5th ed.; M., 1897, II(1), pp. 3-17.

"A Prophetic Career", *British Review*, XII, no. 1 (1915), pp. 3-14.
Transl.: RR, pp. 98-106.

"Rise of the Zemstvos", *The Times Russian Supplement*, 26 April 1915, p. 3.

"The Russian Political Thinker", *The Saturday Review* (7 August 1915), pp. 130-131.
Transl.: RR, pp. 95-97.

"Russia and Europe's War", *New York Times Current History of the European War*, 1:5 (February 1915), pp. 821-825.
Reprint of Letter to *The Times*, 14 September 1914.

Self-Government in Russia. London, Constable, 1915. 118 p. [DLC, MH]
Collection of lectures delivered during the early years of the First World War.

Reprinted: Westport, Connecticut, Hyperion Press, 1979. [DLC]

"The Slavophil Creed", *Hibbert Journal*, XIII (1915), pp. 243-260.

"A Visit to Russia", *Quarterly Review*, no. 443 (1915), pp. 544-554.

«Вопросы национальности в английской публицистике» [Question of Nationality in English News Articles], *Биржевые ведомости* [Stock-Exchange Gazette], no. 14923 (24 June/7 July 1915).
Reprinted: *RR*, pp. 352-359.

1916

«Англия и русские военнопленные» [England and Prisoners of War], *Биржевые ведомости* [Stock-Exchange Gazette], no. 15347 (9/22 February 1916).
Reprinted: *RR*, pp. 360-365.

«Экскурсия на Малабарский берег» [Excursion on the Malabar Coast], Древности (Москва, Московское археологическое общество, 1916), vol. 25, pp. 89-109 [NYPL]

«Экономические теории средневековья» [Economic Theories of Middle Ages], in *История экономической мысли* [History of Economic Thought] (1916), vol. 1, vyp. 3.

"Great Britain and the Russian Prisoners of War", *Khaki* (September 1916), pp. 885-889.

«Максим Максимович Ковалевский. Некролог» [Maksim Maksimovich Kovalevskii. Obituary], *Известия Имп. Академии наук* [News of Imperial Academy of Sciences] (1916), стр. 1163-1170.

Максим Максимович Ковалевский. Некролог. [Maksim Maksimovich Kovalevskii. Obituary]. П., тип. Имп. Академии наук, 1916. 8 стр.

Delivered at the General Meeting of the Imperial Academy of Sciences, 9 May 1916.

«Мечты о мире» [Dreams About Peace], *Биржевые ведомости* [Stock-Exchange Gazette], no. 15456 (22 March/4 April 1916).
Reprinted: RR, pp. 366-376.

"Preface", in Ada Elizabeth Levett (1881-1932) and Adolphus Ballard (1867-1915), *The Black Death*. Reginald Vivian Lennard (1885-19?), *Rural Northamptonshire under the Commonwealth*. Oxford, Clarendon Press, 1916), pp. iii-vii (Oxford Studies in Social and Legal History, 5. Ed. Sir Paul Vinogradoff).

"The Task of Russia", in Winifred Stephens (ed.), *The Soul of Russia*. London, Macmillan and Co., Ltd., 1916, pp. 249-260.

Review of: Howard Levi Gray, *English Field Systems* (London, Humphrey Milford, for Harvard University Press, 1915), ix, 568 p., in *Oxford Magazine* (26 May 1916), pp. 1-4 (offprint pagination).

1917

"The Liberation Movement in Russia", *Manchester Guardian Russian Supplement*, 7 July 1917.
Transl.: RR, pp. 403-406.

"Magna Carta. Cl. 39. *Nullius liber homo, etc.*", in Henry Elliot Malden (ed.), *Magna Carta Commemoration Essays*. Preface by Rt. Hon. Viscount Bruce. [London], Royal Historical Society, 1917, pp. 78-95.

Papers prepared for the celebration to commemorate the seven hundredth anniversary of Magna Carta in June 1915. The First World War prevented the commemoration exercises being held.
Reprinted: *CP*, I, 207-221.

"The Russian Revolution: Its Religious Aspect", *Land and Water* (17 August 1917), pp. 43-44.
  Transl.: *RR*, pp. 407-411.
"Some Elements of the Russian Revolution", *Quarterly Review*, CCXXII, no. 452 (1917), pp. 184-200.
  Transl.: *RR*, pp. 388-402.

"Some Impressions of the Russian Revolution", *The Contemporary Review*, CXI, no. 115 (May 1917), pp. 553-561.
  Transl.: *RR*, pp. 377-387.

"Tasks of the Conference", *The Times*, 28 August 1917.
  Transl.: *RR*, pp. 412-415.

1918

"'The Bolsheviks: A Protest'", *New Europe*, VII, no. 81 (1918), pp. 71-72.

(intro.), Hübner, Rudolf (1864-1945), *A History of Germanic Private Law*, transl. Francis Samuel Philbrick (b. 1876). Preface by Ernest G. Lorenzen. Introductions by Paul Vinogradoff and William Emanuel Walz (b. 1860). Boston, Little, Brown, 1918, pp. xxvii-xxxvi (Continental Legal History Series, vol. 4). [DLC, MH-L]
  Translation of *Grundzüge des deutschen Privatrechts* (2d ed.).
  Reprinted: South Hackensack, New Jersey, Rothman Reprints Inc., 1968.

Историческая основы английского административного права. Речь акад. П. Г. Виноградова, предлочавшаяся к прочтению в торжественном годом собрания Российской Академии наук 29 декабря 1917 г. [Historical Foundations of English Administrative Law. Address of Academician P. G. Vinogradov Prepared for Reading for in the Commemorative Year of the Meeting of the Russian Academy of Sciences on 29 December 1917]. Спб., тип. Российской академии наук, 1918. 55 стр. [РНБ]

«Историческая основы английского административного права. Речь акад. П. Г. Виноградова, предлочавшаяся к прочтению в торжественном годом собрания Российской Академии наук 29 декабря 1917 г.» [Historical Foundations of English Administrative Law. Address of Academician P. G. Vinogradoff Prepared for Reading in the Commemorative Year of the Meeting of the Russian Academy of Sciences on 29 December 1917], *Отчет о деятельности Российской академии наук по Отделениям физико-математических наук и исторических наук и филологии за 1917 г.* [Report on the Activity of the Russian Academy of Sciences for the Divisions of Physical and Mathematical Scinces and Historical Sciences and Philology for 1917] (Спб, изд. Академии наук, 1918), стр. 383-437.

"The Fate of Russia", *The Times*, 22 October 1918.
    Transl.: RR, pp. 420-422.

"The Legal and the Political Aspects of the League of Nations", *The Russian Commonwealth*, I, no. 1 (1 November 1918), pp. 5-9.
    Transl.: RR, pp. 469-475.

"The Manner of Intervention in Russia", *New Europe*, VII, no. 86 (1918), pp. 176-178.

"The Outlook in Russia", *Welsh Outlook* (January 1918), p. 18.
    Transl.: RR, pp. 417-419.

«Реалии Лиги Наций» [Realities of the League of Nations], RR, pp. 476-484.
    Translated and published from the original English-language manuscript version held by the Harvard Law School Archive. Undated.

"Russia and the Future", *Sunday Observer*, 10 March 1918, p. 7.

"Troubled Times in Russian History", *History* (New York, Historical Association, 1918), pp. 1-9.

6 Edward II, A.D. 1312-1313. Ed. P. G. Vinogradoff and L. Ehrlich. London, Quaritch, 1918. liv, 250, 250, 251-281, 3 p. (Publication of the Selden Society, 34). [IHR]

6 Edward II, A.D. 1312-1313. Ed. P. G. Vinogradoff and L. Ehrlich. London, Quaritch, 1918. xl, 130, 130, 131-180 p. (Publication of the Selden Society, 38). [IHR]

Review of: J. Flach (1846-1919), *Les origins de l'ancienne France*. Vol. 4. *Les nationalités regionales. Leurs rapports avec la couronne de France* (Paris, L. Larose et Forcel, 1917), in *Law Quarterly Review*, XXXIV (1918), 211-212.

1919

"Address by Sir Paul Vinogradoff", *The Russian Commonwealth*, I, no. 5-6 (20 January 1919), pp. 146-148.
    Opening Address to a Conference arranged by the Educational Committee of the Russo-British 1917 Bratstvo in London; delivered on 6 January 1919. Vinogradoff was Chairman of the Educational Committee of the Bratstvo.

"The Covenant of the League. Great and Small Powers", *The Times*, 28 March 1919, p. 7.
    Transl.: RR, pp. 485-487.

"The Policy of the Pro-Bolsheviks", *The Russian Commonwealth*, I, no. 9 (15 April 1919), pp. 205-206.

"Prospects in Russia", *Contemporary Review*, CXV (1919), pp. 606-612.
    Transl.: RR, pp. 440-448.

(ed.). *The Reconstruction in Russia*. London, Oxford University Press, 1919. 68 p.

Reprinted: Nendeln, 1975 (Seeds of Conflict; series 4, vol. 3). [MH-L]
Rev: *The Russian Commonwealth*, I, no. 9 (15 April 1919), pp. 227-229 (anon.).

Report of the Educational Conference Held at London, 26 Chester Square 6-8 January 1919. London, Russo-British 1917 Fraternity, 1919. 22 p. [UCL]

"Rusland ved korsveien", *Atlantis*, II (Kristiania, 1919), pp. 67-76.
Transl.: RR, pp. 423-431.

"The Situation in Russia", in P. G. Vinogradoff (ed.), *The Reconstruction in Russia*. London, Oxford University Press, 1919), pp. 7-26.
Transl.: RR, pp. 449-459.

"Western and Eastern Ideals in Russia", *Fortnightly Review*, no. 629 (N.S. 1919), pp. 670-677.
Transl.: RR, pp. 432-439.

1920

"The Crisis of Modern Jurisprudence", *Yale Law Journal*, XXIX (January 1920), 312-320.

The Growth of the Manor (3d rev. ed.; London, George Allen & Unwin, 1920). ix, 384 p. [DLC, MH-L]

Outlines of Historical Jurisprudence. Oxford, Clarendon Press, 1920. [DLC, IHR, MH-L]
Vol. 1. Introduction and Tribal Law.
Rev: *Revue historique de droit*, no. 4 (1924), 726-734 (P. Dareste); *Times Literary Supplement*, 2 December 1920, p. 786; *Athenaeum*, 14 January 1921 (R.R.M.); *Literarische Rundschau*, no. 179 (17 April 1921) (L. Weltmann).
Translation: *Principes historiques du droit. Introduction. Le droit de la tribu*, transl. Paul Duez (1888-1947) and Frédéric Joüon des Longrais (b. 1892). Paris, Payot, 1924. 418 p. [MH-L]

Reprinted: "The Joint Family" (Chapter 6), in *AEL*, pp. 117-128.
Reprinted: "The Organization of Kinship" (Chapter 8), in *AEL*, pp. 57-74.
Reprinted: New York, AMS Press, 1971. [DLC, MH-L]
Reprinted: Holmes Beach, Florida, Gaunt, 1994. [MH-L]
Reprinted: Union, New Jersey, Lawbook Exchange, 1999. [DLC]

Учебник всеобщей истории: [Textbook of Universal History]. Коломеа, Я.Ореншат, [1920]. 3 т.
Древний мир. 232 стр.
Средние века. 248 стр.
Новое время. 304 стр.

Заботы о населении в Англии: сборник статей по вопросам народного образования, воспитания, охране детского труда, общественной медицине, гигене городов и дорожному хозяйству. Со статей П. Г. Виноградова. С предисловием С. П. Тюрина и при участии г.г. сотрудников С. И. Гаврилова. [Concerns About the Population in England: Collection of Articles on Questions of Public Education, Nurturing, Protection of Child Labour, Public Medicine, Hygiene of Cities, and Roads.

1921

"The Legal Background of Demosthenes' Speech in Zenothemis v. Demon", *Revue d'histoire du droit*, III (1921), pp. 163-174.

«Перспективы исторического правоведения» [Prospects for Historical Jurisprudence], *Современные записки* [Contemporary Notes]. [Paris], I, no. 7 (1921), pp. 154-161.

"Preface", in Helen Maud Cam (1885-1968), *Studies in the Hundred Rolls. Some Aspects of Thirteenth Century Administration*. Ludwik Ehrlich (1889-19?), *Proceedings Against the Crown 1216-1377*. (Oxford, Clarendon Press, 1921), pp. iii-x (Oxford Studies in Social and Legal History, 6. Ed. Sir Paul Vinogradoff).

"Russia at the Crossroads", *Contemporary Review*, CXIX (1921), pp. 738-745.
  Transl.: *RR*, pp. 460-468.

Учебник всеобщей истории: Древний мир [Textbook of Universal History: Ancient World]. Stockholm, Северные огни, 1921. 189 стр. [РГБ, РНБ]

"The Work of Rome", in F. S. Marvin (ed.), *The Evolution of World Peace*. London, Edinburgh & Humphrey Milford, Oxford University Press, 1921, pp. 25-42.

Review of: L. Galin, *Justice et systeme penal de la Russie Revolutionnnaire de l'origine au debut du 1920* (Paris, Rousseau et Co., 1920). ix, 120 p. in *Columbia Law Review*, XXI (1921), 730.

1922

"Benckendorff, Alexander", *Encyclopedia Britannica* (12th edn; London, The Encyclopedia Britannica Company, Ltd., 1922), XXX, 447-448.

"Denikin, Anton", *Encyclopedia Britannica* (12th edn; London, The Encyclopedia Britannica Company, Ltd., 1922), XXX, 825-827.

"Guchkov, Alexander", *Encyclopedia Britannica* (London, The Encyclopedia Britannica Company, Ltd., 1922), XXXI, 323.

"Kerensky, Alexander Fedorovich", *Encyclopedia Britannica* (London, The Encyclopedia Britannica Company, Ltd., 1922), XXXI, 680.

"Kolchak, Vladimir Vasilievich", *Encyclopedia Britannica* (12th edn; London, The Encyclopedia Britannica Company, Ltd., 1922), XXXI, 683-684.

"Kornilov, Lavr Georgievich", *Encyclopedia Britannica* (12th edn; London, The Encyclopedia Britannica Company, Ltd., 1922), XXXI, 686-687.

"Lvov, Prince George Eugenievich", *Encyclopedia Britannica* (12th edn; London, The Encyclopedia Britannica Company, Ltd., 1922), XXXI, 812.

"The Meaning of Legal History", *Columbia Law Review*, XXII (December 1922), 693-705.

"Milyukov, Paul Nikolayevich", *Encyclopedia Britannica* (12th edn; London, The Encyclopedia Britannica Company, Ltd., 1922), XXXI, 947.

"Mitteis (1859-1921)", *Journal of Egyptian Archaeology*, VIII, no. 3/4 (October 1922), pp. 258-259.
    Obituary of L. Mitteis.

Outlines of Historical Jurisprudence. Oxford, Clarendon Press, 1922. [DLC, IHR, MH-L]
    Vol. 2. The Jurisprudence of the Greek City.
    Rev: *Revue historique de droit*, no. 4 (1924), pp. 734-739 (B. Haussoullier).
    Reprinted: New York, AMS Press, 1971. [MH-L]
    Reprinted: Holmes Beach, Florida, Gaunt, 1994. [MH-L]
    Reprinted: Union, New Jersey, Lawbook Exchange, 1998.

"Russia", *Encyclopedia Britannica* (12th edn; Cambridge, At the University Press, 1922), XXXII, 309.

"Wrangel, Peter Nicholaievich", *Encyclopedia Britannica* (12th edn; London, The Encyclopedia Britannica Company, Ltd., 1922), XXXII, 1088-1089.

"Yudenich, Nikolai", *Encyclopedia Britannica* (12th edn; London, The Encyclopedia Britannica Company, Ltd., 1922), XXXII, 1112.

1923

Historical Jurisprudence: Introduction (London-New York, Oxford University Press; Humphrey Milford, 1923). 173 p.

Separate publication of the Introduction to Vinogradoff's *Outlines of Historical Jurisprudence*. [MH]

Historical Types of International Law: Lectures Delivered in the University of Leiden. L Leiden, E. J. Brill, 1923. 70 p.
Reprinted: *CP*, II, 248-318.

"Les maxims dans l'ancien droit commun anglais", *Revue historique de droit français et etranger*, II (4th series, 1923), pp. 333-343.
Reprinted: *CP*, II, 239-247.

"Rights of Status in Modern Law", *Canadian Bar Review* (June 1923), pp. 3-12.

"The Roman Elements in Bracton's Treatise", *Yale Law Journal*, XXXII (1923), 751-756.
Reprinted: *CP*, I, 237-244.

Review of: Roscoe Pound (1870-1964), *Interpretations of Legal History* (Cambridge, University Press, 1922), in *English Historical Review*, XXXVIII (1923), 298-299.

1924

"Aims and Methods of Jurisprudence", *Columbia Law Review*, XXIV (January 1924), 1-7.

"Feudalism", in J. B. Bury (ed.), *The Cambridge Medieval History*. New York, Macmillan Pub., 1924), III, pp. 458-484.

"The Foundations of a Theory of Rights", *Yale Law Journal*, XXXIV (November 1924), 60-69.

"The Juridical Nature of the State", *Michigan Law Review*, XXIII (December 1924), 138-153.

"Juridical Persons", *Columbia Law Review*, XXIV (June 1924), 594-604.

"Legal Standards and Ideals", *Michigan Law Review*, XXIII (November 1924), 1-8.

"Preface", in Bertha Haven Putnam (1872-1960), *Early Treatises on the Practice of the Justices of the Peace in the Fifteenth and Sixteenth Centuries*. Oxford, Clarendon Press, 1924), pp. v-vi (Oxford Studies in Social and Legal History, 7. Ed. Sir Paul Vinogradoff).

"Some Problems of Public Law", *California Law Review*, XII (1924), 348-355, 443-453.

1925

Custom and Right. Oslo/Cambridge, Mass., H. Aschehoug & Co. (W. Nygaard)/Harvard University Press, 1925. 3, 109 p. [DLC, MH-L]
 Ten lectures delivered at the Institute of Comparative Research of Culture, Oslo, in 1924.
 Rev.: *Yale Law Journal*, XXXV (1925), 1026-1027 (John M. Zane).
 Reprinted: Union, New Jersey, Lawbook Exchange, 2000. [DLC]
 Reprinted: "Custom and Law", Chapter 2, in *AEL*, pp. 19-30.
 Translation: *Kanshu to kenri*, transl. Michio Aoyama (b. 1902). Tokyo, Iwanami-shoten, 1934. 138, 13 p. [MH-L]

"Preface", in Ernest Fraser Jacob (1894-1971), *Studies in the Period of Baronial Reform and Rebellion (1258-1267)*. Oxford, Clarendon Press,

1925), pp. v-x (Oxford Studies in Social and Legal History, 8. Ed. Sir Paul Vinogradoff).
    Reprinted: New York, Octagon Books, 1974. 443 p.

"Ralph of Hengham as Chief Justice of the Common Pleas", in A. G. Little and F. M. Powicke (ed.), *Essays in Medieval History Presented to Thomas Frederick Tout*. Manchester, 1925, pp. 189-196.
    Reprinted: *CP*, I, 245-252.

"Some Considerations on the Methods of Ascertaining Legal Customs", in *Księgi pamiatkowej ku ezci Oswalda Balzera*. Lviv, Z drukami zakladu narodowego im. Osslinskich, 1925. 12 p.

1926

"Customary Law", in Charles George Crump (1862-1935) and Ernest Fraser Jacob (1894-1971) (eds.), *Legacy of the Middle Ages*. Oxford, Clarendon Press, 1926, pp. --.
    Reprinted: Oxford, Clarendon Press, 1932. xii, 549 p. (with corrections)
    Reprinted: Oxford, Clarendon Press, 1938. xii, 549 p.
    Reprinted: Oxford, Clarendon Press, 1948. xii, 548 p.
    Reprinted: Oxford, Clarendon Press, [1951]. xii, 548 p.

"Quelques problèmes d'histoire du droit anglo-normand", *Revue historique de droit français et étranger*, v (4th series, 1926), 195-212.
    Reprinted: *CP*, II, 423-437.

Select Cases to Illustrate the History of English Land Law. Oxford, printed for private circulation, 1926. 56 p. [Oxford]

1927

[David Charles Douglas (1898-1982)], *The Social Structure of Medieval East Anglia*. Preface by H. W. C. Davis. Oxford, Clarendon Press,

1927. (Oxford Studies in Social and Legal History, 9. Ed. Sir Paul Vinogradoff)].

1928

The Collected Papers of Paul Vinogradoff. With a Memoir by the Right Hon. H. A. L. Fisher. Oxford, Clarendon Press, 1928. 2 vols.
 Reprinted: London, Wildy & Sons, 1963. 2 vols.
 Reprinted: New York, Gryphon Legal Classics, 1995. 2 vols.

"The Problem of Customary Law", *Acta Academiae Universalis Jurisprudentiae Comparativae*, I (1928), pp. 231-243. [MH-L]

1958

"al-Nizam al-iqta" [The Feudal System], in *al-Iqta wa-al-'usur al-wusta fi gharb Uruba*, Arabic transl. Muhammed Mustafa Ziyadah. 3d ed. Cairo, Maktabat al-Nahdah al-Misriyah, 1958. xvi, 140, p. 10 illus. [SOAS]
 Arabic translation of a work by Vinogradoff not identified, together with a reprint of an article by George Coopland on feudalism in the Middle Ages.

1962

«Из писем П. Г. Виноградова» [From the Letters of P. G. Vinogradoff], *Средние века* [Middle Ages], вып. XXII (1962), стр. 265-282.
 Edited with preface and commentary of K. A. Maikova.

1991

«"За" и "против" республики» ["For" and "Against" a Republic], *Исторический архив* [Historical Archive], № 2 (1991), стр. 53-62.
 With preface and commentary of A. V. Antoshchenko.

1997

«Россия и Европа» [Russia and Europe], *Исторический архив* [Historical Archive], № 1 (1997), стр. 201-216; № 2, стр. 208-209,

2000

«Каждый должен бороться на своем месте: Письма П. Г. Виноградова к П. Б. Струве. 1902-1904» [Each should Struggle for His Own Place: Letters of P G. Vinogradoff to P. V. Struve. 1902-1904], *Исторический архив* [Historical Archive], № 5 (2000), стр. 186-201.
With preface by A. V. Antoshchenko.

«Неопубликованные страницы третьего тома «Очерки исторического правоведения» П. Г. Виноградова. Публичное выступление и комментарий А. В. Антощенко» [Unpublished Pages of Volume Three of "Outlines of Historical Jurisprudence" of P. G. Vinogradoff. Public Address and Commentary of A. V. Antoshchenko], *Средние века* [Middle Ages]. М., Наука, 2000, вып. 61, стр. 289-313 [МПГУ]

2001

«Письма академика П. Г. Виноградова И. В. Шкловскому (Дионео)» [Letters of Academician P. G. Vinogradoff to I. V. Shklovskii (Dioneo)], *История и историки: Историграфический вестник* [History and Historians: Historiographical Gazette] (М., Наука, 2001), стр. 317-325.

2002

«Мы в созвездии политических волнений»: Письма П. Г. Виноградова В. И. Вернадскому. 1899-1904 гг.» ["We are in a Constellation of Political Disturbances": Letters of P. G. Vinogradoff to V. I. Vernadskii. 1899-1904], *Исторический архив* [Historical Archive], № 2 (2002), стр. 129-141.
 Prepared and edited by A. V. Antoshchenko.

2004

«О прогрессе» [On Progress], *Журнал социологии и социальной антропологии* [Journal of Sociology and Social Anthropology], VII, № 4 (2004), стр. 129-141.

2008

Россия на распутье. Историко-публицистические статьи [Russia at the Crossroads], Compiled, Preface, and Commentary by A. V. Antoshchenko. Transl. from English by A. V. Antoshchenko and A. V. Golubeva; transl. from Norwegian by O. N. Sannikova (M., Издательский дом «Территория будущего», 2008). 576 p.

Publications Untraced

The following publications have been identified as having been written by Sir Paul Vinogradoff on the basis of offprints and/or manuscript materials in the Vinogradoff archives, but further details are lacking:

«Годичные книги английский судов, как исторический источник», pp. 427-434 (no source indicated).

«Задачи всеобщей истории: Отрывок из университетского курса Грановского», pp. 308-324. (journal not specified).

"Осбьерн-Тюленья смерть», Детский отдых, pp. 106-123

II. Приложения к протоколам заседаний 2-ой под-группы пятой группы. 1. Доклад ордин. Профессора П. Г. Виноградова: учебный план и программа истории. Pp. 61-64. (no place of publication indicated)

Personal Archives

Harvard Law School, Cambridge, Massachusetts
Moscow Lomonosov State University, Russian Federation

Vinogradoff papers also repose in the Personal Archive of Igor Pavlovich Vinogradoff (1901-1987), held at Leeds University, England.

Selected Personalia

Allen, Carleton Kemp. "Vinogradoff, Sir Paul", *Dictionary of National Biography 1922-1930* (London, Oxford University Press, 1937), pp. 871-874.

Antoshchenko, A. V. «О формировании политической программы П. Г. Виноградова» [On Forming the Political Program of P. G. Vinogradov], in *Исторический ежегодник. Специальный выпуск* [Historical Yearbook. Special Issue. 2000] (Omsk, 2001), pp. 78-91.

Antoshchenko, A. V. «Об общественной деятельности П. Г. Виноградова» [On the Social Activity of P. G. Vinogradoff], *Общество и жизнь* [Society and Power] (Spb., 2001), I, pp. 15-31.

Antoshchenko, A. V. «П. Г. Виноградов об университетском вопросе в России на рубеже XIX-XX вв. [P. G. Vinogradoff on the University Question in Russia at the Turn of the Nineteenth-Twentieth Centuries], *Русская наука в биографических очерках* [Russian Science in Biographical Sketches] (Spb., 2003), pp. 200-220.

Antoshchenko, A. V. «Политическая позиция П. Г. Виноградова в годы первой русской революции» [Political Position of P. G. Vinogradoff in the Years of the First Russian Revolution], *Проблемы российской истории* [Problems of Russian History] (M., Magnitogorsk, 2007), VIII, pp. 61-78.

Antoshchenko, A. V. «Россия на переломе (о проблемах российской истории в публицистике П. Г. Виноградова)» [Russia in Crisis (On the Problems of Russian History of the Publicist Writings of P. G. Vinogradoff], in *RR*, pp. 9-46.

Barnes, Thomas G. "Introduction", *The Collected Papers of Paul Vinogradoff*. [Delran, New Jersey], Gryphon Editions, 1995. 30 p.
   Booklet accompanying the Gryphon Editions "Legal Classics Library" as "Notes from the Editors".

Fisher, Herbert Albert Laurens (1865-1940). *Paul Vinogradoff. A Memoir*. Oxford, The Clarendon Press, 1927. 74 p. [MH-L]
   Reprinted: *CP*, I, pp. 1-74. [MH-L]

Glebov, A. G. *Проблемы истории английского средневекового крестьянства в творчестве П. Г. Виноградова* [Problems of the History of the English Medieval Peasantry in the Work of P. G. Vinogradoff]. М., 1990. (МГУ им. М. В. Ломоносова. Исторический факультет. Кафедра истории средних веков). 24 р. [РНБ]

Holdsworth, Sir William Searle (1871-1944). "Professor Sir Paul Vinogradoff. 1854-1925", *Proceedings of The British Academy*, XI (1924-25), 486-501.

Holdsworth, Sir William Searle, *The Historians of Anglo-American Law*. New York, Oxford University Press, 1928, pp. 84-91.
   Reprinted: Union, New Jersey, Lawbook Exchange Ltd., 1994. ii, 176 p.

Holdsworth, Sir William Searle. "Professor Sir Paul Vinogradoff (1854-1925)", *Proceedings of The British Academy* (London, British Academy, [1926]. 16 p. [MH-L]

Holdsworth, Sir William Searle and Pares, Sir Bernard (1867-1949). *Slavonic Review*, IV (1926), 529-551.
Maklakov, Basil, "Vinogradov", *Slavonic Review*, XIII (1935), 633-640.

Moiseenkova, L. S. *Патриарх российской медиевистики: жизнь и научное творчество П. Г. Виноградова* [Patriarch of Russian Medieval Studies: Life and Scholarly Work of P. G. Vinogradoff]. Симферополь, Реноме, 2000. 181 стр.

Moiseenkova, L. S. *П. Г. Виноградов как историк средних вековой Англии* [Vinogradoff as an Historian of the Middle Ages of England] Казань, 1987. 19 стр. [РНБ]

Parker, C. "Paul Vinogradoff, the Delusions of Russian Liberalism, and the Development of Russian Studies in England", *Slavonic and East European Review*, LXIX (1991), 42.

Petrushevskii, Dmitrii (1863-1942). *П. Г. Виноградов как социальный историк* [P. G. Vinogradoff as a Social Historian], ed. V. I. Vernadskii and I. Iu. Krachkovskii. Ленинград, изд-во Академии наук СССР. 1930. 27 стр. (Труды Комиссии по истории знания, 9) [МН, РНБ]

Polianskii, F., «О русских буржуазных историках английской деревни» [On Russian Bourgeois Historians of the English Village], *Вопросы истории* [Questions of History], no. 3 (1949), pp. 93-107.
  On M. M. Kovalevskii, P. Vinogradoff, I. Granat, and D. M. Petrushevskii.

Powicke, Frederick M. (1879-1963). "Sir Paul Vinogradoff", *English Historical Review*, XLI (1926), 236-243.

Powicke, Frederick M. "Sir Paul Vinogradoff", in *Modern Historians and the Study of History: Essays and Papers* (London, 1935), I, pp. 9-18.

Sargeant, E. "Russian Liberalism versus Bolshevism: The Debate Between Vinogradoff and Lenin (1905-1907)", *International Politics*, XXXIII (1996), pp. 341-371.

Schechter, T. I. "Paul Vinogradoff – the Pontiff of Comparative Jurisprudence", *Illinois Law Review*, XXIV (1929-30), pp. 528-546.

Seagle, William, "Sir Paul Vinogradoff (1854-1925)", *Encyclopedia of the Social Sciences*, ed. E. R. A. Seligman (New York, Macmillan, 1935), vol. XV, pp. 263-264.

Sir Paul Vinogradoff. London, Eyre & Spottiswood, 1926. 36 p. [MH-L]

Contains reprints of notices by Sir William S. Holdsworth, Sir Bernard Pares (1867-1949), and Baron Alexander Feliksovich Meyendorff (1869-1964) of Vinogradoff's death.

Stein, Peter. "Vinogradoff, Sir Paul Gavrilovitch", *Oxford Dictionary of National Biography*, ed. H. C. G. Matthew and B. Harrison. (Oxford, Oxford University Press, 2004), LVI, 553-555.

"Vinogradoff, Paul", in *Encyclopedia Britannica* (11th ed.; Cambridge, at the University Press, 1910-11), XXVIII, p. 100.

Zulueta, Francis de (1878-1958). "Paul Vinogradoff, 1854-1925", *Law Quarterly Review*, XLII (1926), 202-211.

www.ingramcontent.com/pod-product-compliance
Lightning Source LLC
Chambersburg PA
CBHW022013300426
44117CB00005B/161